EACL Workshop on Computational Approaches to Semitic Languages 2009

Held in Conjunction with EACL 2009

Athens, Greece
31 March 2009

ISBN: 978-1-61738-562-9

Printed from e-media with permission by:

Curran Associates, Inc.
57 Morehouse Lane
Red Hook, NY 12571
www.proceedings.com

Some format issues inherent in the e-media version may also appear in this print version.

Printed by Curran Associates, Inc. (2010)

Association for Computational Linguistics
209 N. Eighth Street
Stroudsburg, Pennsylvania 18360

Phone: 1-570-476-8006
Fax: 1-570-476-0860

acl@aclweb.org

Preface

We are delighted to present you with this volume containing the papers accepted for presentation at the EACL 2009 Workshop on Computational Approaches to Semitic Languages, held in Athens, Greece, on March 31st, 2009.

The Workshop is an opportunity for the ACL Special Interest Group on Computational Approaches to Semitic Languages to meet and discuss current and future directions in Computational Linguistic and Natural Language Processing approaches to Semitic Languages. Previous workshops took place in 1998 (Montreal), 2002 (Philadelphia), 2005 (Ann Arbor) and 2007 (Prague). We are happy to see more, better submissions every year. This year we received 19 submissions, of which 9 were selected for presentation and are included in this volume. These papers address Arabic (both standard and dialectal), Hebrew and Ancient Syriac, as well as general issues pertaining to all Semitic languages. We are privileged to have Prof. Michael Gasser (Indiana University) as our keynote speaker this year. Professor Gasser will talk on Finite state morphology for Ethiopian Semitic languages.

We are extremely grateful to the members of the Program Committee who reviewed the submissions and helped shape up the Program: Ann Bies (LDC, University of Pennsylvania, USA), Tim Buckwalter (University of Maryland, USA), Violetta Cavalli-Sforza (Carnegie Mellon University, USA), Joseph Dichy (University of Lyon 2, France), Michael Elhadad (Ben Gurion University, Israel), Martha W. Evens (Illinois Institute of Technology, USA), Ray Fabri (University of Malta), Ali Farghaly (Oracle, USA), Alexander Fraser (University of Stuttgart, Germany), Andrew Freeman (Washington University, USA), Albert Gatt (University of Aberdeen, UK), Gregory Grefenstette, (Exalead, France), Nizar Habash (Columbia University, USA), Alon Itai (Technion, Israel), Steven Krauwer (Utrecht University, Netherlands), Mohamed Maamouri (LDC, University of Pennsylvania USA), Bente Maegaard (CST, University of Copenhagen, Denmark), Nurit Melnik (Oranim College, Israel), Uzzi Ornan (Technion, Israel), Owen Rambow (Columbia University, USA), Paolo Rosso (Universidad Politecnica Valencia, Spain), Khalil Sima'an (University of Amsterdam, Netherlands), Abdelhadi Soudi (Ecole Nationale de l'Industrie Minerale, Morocco), Adam Ussishkin (University of Arizona, USA), and Imed Zitouni (IBM Research, USA)

Above all, we would like to thank the authors and the participants of the Workshop. We hope you have a very enjoyable and productive time in Athens!

Mike Rosner and Shuly Wintner
Program Committee Chairs

Table of Contents

Conference Program

Tuesday, March 31, 2009

9:00–10:00 Opening Remarks and Invited Talk by Michael Gasser

Session 1: Philology

10:00–10:30 *How to Establish a Verbal Paradigm on the Basis of Ancient Syriac Manuscripts*
Wido van Peursen

Session 2: Morphology

11:00–11:30 *The Karamel System and Semitic Languages: Structured Multi-Tiered Morphology*
François Barthélemy

11:30–12:00 *Revisiting Multi-Tape Automata for Semitic Morphological Analysis and Generation*
Mans Hulden

12:00–12:30 *A Hybrid Approach for Building Arabic Diacritizer*
Khaled Shaalan, Hitham M. Abo Bakr and Ibrahim Ziedan

Session 3: Applications

14:30–15:00 *Unsupervised Concept Discovery In Hebrew Using Simple Unsupervised Word Prefix Segmentation for Hebrew and Arabic*
Elad Dinur, Dmitry Davidov and Ari Rappoport

15:00–15:30 *Automatic Treebank-Based Acquisition of Arabic LFG Dependency Structures*
Lamia Tounsi, Mohammed Attia and Josef van Genabith

15:30–16:00 *Spoken Arabic Dialect Identification Using Phonotactic Modeling*
Fadi Biadsy, Julia Hirschberg and Nizar Habash

Tuesday, March 31, 2009 (continued)

Session 4: Applications

16:30–17:00 *Structure-Based Evaluation of an Arabic Semantic Query Expansion Using the JIRS Passage Retrieval System*
Lahsen Abouenour, Karim Bouzoubaa and Paolo Rosso

17:00–17:30 *Syntactic Reordering for English-Arabic Phrase-Based Machine Translation*
Jakob Elming and Nizar Habash

Closing

17:30–18:00 Discussion and final remarks

How to Establish a Verbal Paradigm on the Basis of Ancient Syriac Manuscripts

W.Th. (Wido) van Peursen
Leiden Institute for Religious Studies
P.O. Box 9515
NL-2300 RA Leiden
w.t.van.peursen@religion.leidenuniv.nl

Abstract

This paper describes a model that has been developed in the Turgama Project at Leiden University to meet the challenges encountered in the computational analysis of ancient Syriac Biblical manuscripts. The small size of the corpus, the absence of native speakers, and the variation attested in the multitude of textual witnesses require a model of encoding—rather than tagging—that moves from the formal distributional registration of linguistic elements to functional deductions. The model is illuminated by an example from verb inflection. It shows how a corpus-based analysis can improve upon the inflectional paradigms given in traditional grammars and how the various orthographic representations can be accounted for by an encoding system that registers both the paradigmatic forms and their attested realizations.

1 Working with ancient documents

1.1 Challenges

If we wish to make a linguistic analysis of ancient texts, in our case the Hebrew Bible and its Syriac translation, the Peshitta (ca. 2nd century CE), we are confronted with a number of challenges:

- There is no native speaker of the languages involved. We do not know in advance what categories are relevant in the linguistic analysis, what functions a certain construction has, or what functional oppositions there exist in the language system. For this reason we should avoid as much as we can any model that presupposes knowledge about the language.
- We have only written sources. Hence we are challenged by the complex interaction between orthographic conventions and morphological phenomena. There are even some orthographic practices which, it is claimed, have never been supported by a phonological or morphological realization (see section 4.5).
- We are dealing with multiple unique documents. In philology, *the* text of the Hebrew Bible or its Syriac translation is an abstract notion, a scholarly construct. The corpus that we enter into our database consists of the concrete *witnesses* to the abstract text. Textual variants provide useful information about language variation and development (section 4.5).
- We are dealing with a small corpus. The Hebrew Bible contains about 300.000–400.000 words (depending on whether we count graphic words or functional words); the vocabulary consists of about 8.000 lexemes.

Moreover, because of the context in which our research takes place, at the boundary of linguistics and philology, our aim is the construction of a database with a correctly encoded text. Because we want to understand the text, rather than merely collect knowledge about the language system, we have set high standards of accuracy for the encoding of the text.

1.2 Dilemmas

These challenges lead to the following dilemmas for the computational analysis of ancient texts:

- Data-oriented or theory-driven? Since approaches that presuppose linguistic knowledge are problematic, we want to be

Proceedings of the EACL 2009 Workshop on Computational Approaches to Semitic Languages, pages 1–9,
Athens, Greece, 31 March, 2009. ©2009 Association for Computational Linguistics

data-oriented, rather than theory-driven. However, approaches that merely try to extract knowledge from the corpus with a minimum of human input are insufficient because of the size of our corpus and because we want knowledge about the text, not just about the language.

- Priority for the corpus or the language? Due to the lack of native speakers, the sole basis for our knowledge about the language is the corpus, but, at the same time, the corpus can only be accessed through some linguistic knowledge and some basic understanding of the text. We cannot start from scratch, avoiding any preliminary understanding of the text, its language, its features, and its meaning. This understanding is shaped by our scholarly and cultural tradition. It is based on transmitted knowledge. But we have to find ways in which the computational analysis does not only imitate or repeat traditional interpretations.

1.3 Requirements

The challenges and dilemmas mentioned above require a model that is deductive rather than inductive; that goes from form (the concrete textual data) to function (the categories that we do not know a priori); that entails registering the distribution of linguistic elements, rather than merely adding functional labels—in other words, that involves encoding rather than tagging; that registers both the paradigmatic forms and their realizations; that allows grammatical categories and formal descriptions to be redefined on the basis of corpus analysis; and that involves interactive analytical procedures, which are needed for the level of accuracy we aim for.

In the distributional analysis at word level, for example, we mark prefixes and suffixes, rather than tagging a form as "imperfect 2ms" etc. Similarly on clause level we identify patterns such as "subject + participle + complement", as against the usual practice of giving functional clause labels such as "circumstantial clause".

2 Analytical procedure

In our project the analysis of Hebrew and Syriac involves a bottom-up linguistic analysis at the following levels:

2.1 Word level

This level concerns the segmentation of words into morphemes, the functional deductions from the morphological analysis, and the assignment of lexically determined word functions. It will be described in detail in section 3.

2.2 Phrase level

At this level words are combined into phrases (e.g. noun + adjective). This entails the morphosyntactic analysis and the systematic adaptations of word classes in certain environments (e.g. adjective → noun), and the analysis of phrase-internal relations (e.g. apposition).

2.3 Clause level

This level concerns the combination of phrases into clauses (e.g. conjunction + VP + determinate NP), and the assignment of syntactic functions (e.g. subject, predicate).

2.4 Text level

This level concerns the determination of the relationships between clauses and the assignment of the syntactical functions of the clauses within the text hierarchy (e.g. object clause).

3 Workflow of word-level analysis

In the following discussion we will restrict ourselves to the morphological analysis. At the higher linguistic levels the same principles are applied, although the consequences are somewhat different (see section 5).

3.1 Running text

As an example we take the Syriac translation (Peshitta) of the book of Judges. The starting-point of the analysis is a transliterated running text, called P_Judges, which reflects the Leiden Peshitta edition. Sample 1 contains the first verse of this text. The variant notation between square brackets indicates that the first word, `whw'`, 'and it happened', is missing in a number of manuscripts. Between the angle brackets a comment has been added.

Even this first step involves a number of disambiguating decisions, for example, as to whether a dot above a letter is a vowel sign, a delimitation marker, or just a spot in the manuscript.[1]

[1] One has to take similar decisions if one transcribes the text of a manuscript to Unicode, because the definitions of the Unicode characters include both a for-

```
1 [whw'/ -6h7, 8a1c, 10c1, 11c1, 12a1fam]
<check reading in 6h7> mn btr dmyt y$w` brnwn
`bdh dmry'; 1 $'lw bn:y 'ysryl bmry' w'mr:yn;
mnw nsq ln `l kn`n:y' bry$'; lmtkt$w `mhwn
bqrb';
```

Sample 1: P_Judges (running text)

3.2 Production of graphic text ('pil2wit')

The program pil2wit transforms the running text into the so-called graphic text, a transliterated text according to an established format that enables the subsequent steps in the analysis (sample 2). It has another transliteration system;[2] instructions to select variants have been executed; comments have been omitted; and the markers of book, chapter and verse have been added.

```
  1  %bookname Jd
  2  %language syriac
  3
  4  %verse 1,1
  5    WHW> MN BTR DMJT JCW< BRNWN <BDH DMRJ>
C>LW BN"J >JSRJL BMRJ> W>MR"JN MNW NSQ LN <L
KN<N"J> BRJC> LMTKTCW <MHWN BQRB>
```

Sample 2: P_Judices (graphic text)

3.3 Production of encoded text ('Analyse')

The grapic text is the input file for the program Analyse, which concerns the segmentation of the Syriac words into morphemes (as far as concatenative morphemes are involved[3]). For this segmentation we use a system of encoding, rather than tagging. Thus the imperfect form *neqtol* "he will kill" is encoded as `!N!QV&WL[`, in which the exclamation marks `!...!` indicate the prefix, the ampersand `&` a paradigmatically unexpected letter—the round bracket `(` indicates an expected but absent letter—and the square bracket to the right `[` a verbal ending. Sample 3 provides the interface in the interactive procedure of Analyse.

```
1,1 WHW>      W-HW(J&>[, W-HW(J&>[/
1,1 MN        MN, MN=
1,1 BTR       BTR
1,1 DMJT      D-M(W&JT[, D-M(W&JT[/:p
1,1 JCW<      JCW</
1,1 BRNWN     BR/-NWN=/
1,1 <BDH      <BD=/-H, <BD[-H, <BD==/-H
1,1 DMRJ>     D-MRJ>/
```

Sample 3: P_Judices.an (analysed text; automatically generated file)

The first column contains the verse number, the second the graphic words (which may contain more than one functional word; thus the first graphic word contains the conjunction `W` and the verb `HW>`) and the third column contains proposals for the morphological segmentation. These proposals are generated from the 'Analytical Lexicon', a data file containing the results of previous analyses (sample 4).

```
9308  WCKR>     W-CKR/~>
9309  WCLWM     W-CLWM/
9310  WCLX      W-CLX[
9311  WCLX      W-CLX[(W
9312  WCLXW     W-CLX[W
9313  WCLXT     W-CLX[T==
```

Sample 4: Excerpt from the Analytical Lexicon

It appears, for example, that up to the moment that sample 4 was extracted from the lexicon, the form `WCLX` had received two different encodings (lines 9310 and 9311; see below, section 4.3).

The human researcher has to accept or reject the proposals made by Analyse or to add a new analysis. We cannot go through all details, but in the second line of sample 4, for example, a choice has to be made between the preposition *men* (`MN`) and the interrogative pronoun *man* (`MN=`; the disambiguating function of the equals sign is recorded in the lexicon [section 3.6], where both `MN` and `MN=` are defined). Likewise, in the case of `<BDH`, the human researcher has to decide whether this is a verb (hence the verbal ending `[`), the noun 'servant' (`<BD=`), or the noun 'work' (`<BD==`).

For these disambiguating decisions in the interactive procedure the human researcher follows a protocol that describes the relative weight of diacritical dots in the oldest manuscripts, the vowel signs that are added in some manuscripts, the vocalization in printed editions, and grammatical and contextual considerations.

```
1,1 WHW>        W-HW(J&>[
1,1 MN          MN
1,1 BTR         BTR
1,1 DMJT        D-M(W&JT[
1,1 JCW<        JCW</
1,1 BRNWN       BR/-NWN=/
1,1 <BDH        <BD=/-H
1,1 DMRJ>       D-MRJ>/
```

Sample 5: P_Judices.an (analysed text; outcome of interactive procedure)

After the interactive procedure the analysed text contains the 'correct' analysis for each word of

---

mal description and a functional analysis. There is not a character for 'a dot above the letter', but rather for 'vowel sign above the letter' etc.

[2] Transliteration alphabet: > B G D H W Z X V J K L M N S < P Y Q R C T.

[3] Non-concatenative morphemes are marked with a colon at the end of a word. We use `:p` for the vowel pattern of the passive; `:d` for the doubled verbal stem and `:c` for the construct state vocalization of nouns.

the graphic text (sample 5). As we shall see below, we do not consider this as the definitive analysis, but rather as a hypothesis about the data that can be tested in the following steps of the analytical procedure.

3.4 Reformatting and selection ('Genat')

The next step concerns the selection of a chapter and the reformatting of the document. This is done automatically by the program Genat. The result is e.g. P_Judices01.at (sample 6).

```
1,1  W-HW(J&>[ MN BTR D-M(W&JT[ JCW</ BR/-
NWN=/ <BD=/-H D-MRJ>/ C>L[W BN/J >JSRJL/ B-
MRJ>/ W->MR[/JN MN=-(HW !N!S(LQ[ L-N <L
KN<NJ/(J~> B-RJC/~> L-!M!@(>T@KTC[/W:d <M-
HWN= B-QRB=/~>
```

Sample 6: P_Judices01.at (analysed text, reformatted)

3.5 Functional deductions ('at2ps')

The next step concerns the functional deductions from the morphological analysis (e.g. person, number, gender) and the assignment of lexically determined word functions (e.g. part of speech). For this purpose the program at2ps uses three language definition files: a description of the alphabet, a lexicon (section 3.6), and a description of the morphology ('Word Grammar'; section 3.7).

3.6 The Lexicon

Each line in the Lexicon contains the lexeme, a unique identification number, lexically relevant characteristics such as a part of speech (`sp`) or a lexical set (`ls`), a gloss (`gl`), which is only intended for the human user and, optionally, a comment added after the hash (#).

```
CLWM    6577:sp=subs:ls=prop:st=abs:gn=m:gl=
        Shallum
CLX     10753:sp=verb:gl=to send, PA to strip,
        to despoil
CLX=    15359:sp=subs:ls=prop:st=abs:gn=m:gl=
        Shilhi
CLX==   32679:sp=subs:de=CLX>:gl=swarm (bees),
        skin (lamb)        # Judges 14,08
```

Sample 7: Extract from the Lexicon

3.7 The 'Word Grammar'

The encoded text is read by the Word Grammar. In this auxiliary file are registered (1) the types of morphemes recognized; (2) the individual morphemes of each morpheme type; (3) a list of grammatical functions; and (4) rules for the functional deductions (see samples 8–11).

```
prefix =
    pfm:  {"!","!"} "preformative"
    pfx:  {"@","@"} "passive stem formation
          prefix"
    vbs:  {"]","]"} "verbal stem"
core =
    lex:  {} "lexeme"
suffix =
    vbe:  {"["} "verbal ending"
    nme:  {"/"} "nominal ending"
    emf:  {"~"} "emphatic marker"
pattern =
    vpm:  {":"} "vowel pattern"
functions
ps: "person" =
    first: "first", second: "second", third:
    "third"
nu: "number" =
    sg: "singular", du: "dual", pl: "plural",
    unknown: "unknown"
gn: "gender" =
    f: "feminine", m: "masculine"
```

Sample 8: Extract from the Word Grammar, section 1: Morpheme types

```
vbe =   "",    "W",    "WN",    "J",    "J=",    "JN",
        "JN=",   "N",   "N=",   "T",   "T=",   "T==",
        "TWN",  "TJ",  "TJN"
```

Sample 9: Extract from Word Grammar, section 2: Individual morphemes for morpheme types

```
ps: "person" =
    first: "first", second: "second", third:
    "third"
nu: "number" =
    sg: "singular", du: "dual", pl: "plural",
    unknown: "unknown"
gn: "gender" =
    f: "feminine", m: "masculine"
```

Sample 10: Extract from the Word Grammar, section 3: Grammatical functions

```
shared { exist(pfm) && exist(vbe) && not ex-
    ist(nme) :: vt=ipf }
    shared { pfm == "N" :: ps=third }
        vbe == "" :: gn=m, nu=sg
        vbe != {"", "WN", "N="} :: reject
    end
shared { pfm == "T=" :: ps=third }
        vbe == {""} :: gn=f, nu=sg
                vbe != "" :: reject
    end
```

Sample 11: Extract from the Word Grammar, section 4: Rules for functional deductions

Each rule concerns the pairing of a morphological condition and an action. The condition is phrased as a Boolean expression yielding true or false indicating whether the condition is met or not. If the condition is met, the listed actions are undertaken. An action is usually the assignment of a value to a word function, but can also involve accepting or rejecting a form, or jumping to a rule further down. Thus the rule

```
vbe == "W"    :: gn=m, nu=pl
```

can be read as: *if* there is a verbal ending `W`, *then* assign the values gender = masculine and number = plural.

3.8 Result: the ps2 file

The result is a ps2 file. Each row contains a verse reference, the lexeme, and a list of lexical and morphological features such as the lexical set, part of speech, verbal prefix, verbal stem, verbal ending, nominal ending, verbal tense, person, number, gender, nominal state. Thus the second line of sample 12 shows that the second word of Judges is `HWJ`, 'to be', which has the lexical set 'verb of existence' (`-2`); it has the part of speech 'verb' (`1`); it has no verbal prefix (`0`); it comes from the simple verbal stem Peal or Qal (`0`); it has an empty verbal ending (`1`); it has no nominal ending (`0`); it is a perfect form (`2`) 3rd person (`3`) singular (`1`), without personal suffix (`-1`),[4] masculine (`2`); and the notion of 'state' does not apply to it (`-1`), because this notion is only used in the case of nominal endings.

```
01,01 W     0    6 -1 -1 -1 -1 -1   -1 -1 -1 -1    -1
01,01 HWJ -2    1  0  0  1  0 -1    2  3  1  2    -1
01,01 MN    0    5 -1 -1 -1 -1 -1   -1 -1 -1 -1    -1
01,01 BTR   0    5 -1 -1 -1 -1 -1   -1 -1 -1 -1    -1
01,01 D    -1    5 -1 -1 -1 -1 -1   -1 -1 -1 -1    -1
01,01 MWT   0    1  0  0  1  0 -1    2  3  1  2    -1
01,01 JCW< 0    3 -1 -1 -1  1 -1   -1 -1  0  2     2
01,01 BR    0    2 -1 -1 -1  1 -1   -1 -1  0  2     0
01,01 NWN= 0    3 -1 -1 -1  1 -1   -1 -1  0  2     2
```

Sample 12: P_Judices.ps2

From this file two files are automatically generated: an encoded surface text (xxx.ct) and a data description in human readable form (xxx.dmp).

```
1  RICHT01,01 W-HW> MN BTR D-MJT JCW< BR-NWN
<BD-H D-MRJ> C>LW BNJ >JSRJL B-MRJ> W->MRJN
MN-W NSQ L-N <L KN<NJ> B-RJC> L-MTKTCW <M-HWN
B-QRB> *
```

Sample 13: P_Judices01.ct

```
1,1 W          W    W     sp=conj
1,1 HW(J&>[  HW>  HWJ   vbe="",sp=verb,vo=act,vs=pe,
                          vt=pf,ps=third,nu=sg,gn=m,
                          ls=vbex
1,1 MN         MN   MN    sp=prep
1,1 BTR        BTR  BTR   sp=prep
1,1 D          D    D     ls=pcon,sp=prep
1,1 M(W&JT[  MJT  MWT   vbe="" sp=verb,vo=act,vs=pe,
                          vt=pf,ps=third,nu=sg,gn=m
1,1 JCW</     JCW< JCW< nme="" sp=subs,+nu,gn=m,st=
                          abs,ls=prop
1,1 BR/        BR   BR    nme="" sp=subs,+nu,gn=m,+st
1,1 NWN=/     NWN  NWN=  nme="" sp=subs,+nu,gn=m,st=
                          abs,ls=prop
```

Sample 14: P_Judices01.dmp

[4] This column comes from an earlier phase of our project. In our present encoding the value is always 'inapplicable' (`-1`), because we now treat the suffix pronoun as an independent lexeme. Its lexeme status appears from its own grammatical functions, which are different from those of the word to which it is attached. The traditional lexicographical practice, however, does not treat it as a lexeme (Sikkel, 2008).

3.9 Summary of the workflow

The workflow can be summarized as follows:

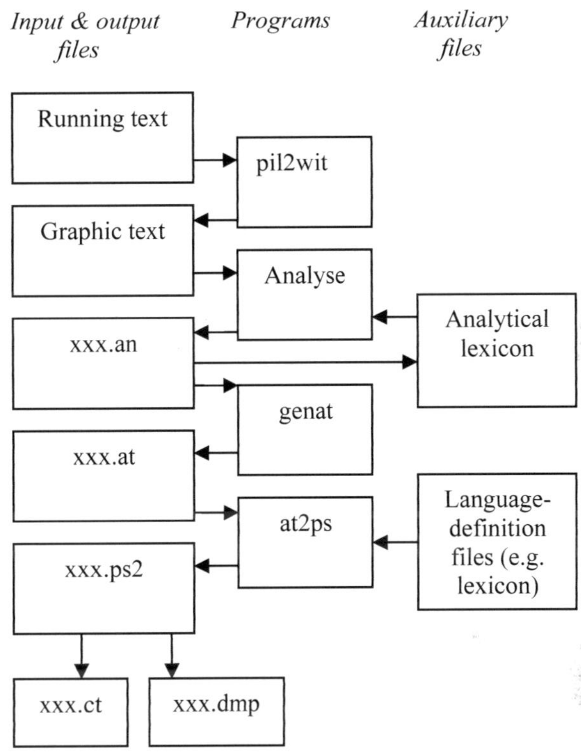

Table 1: workflow of word level analysis

It follows that the following programs and data sets are used:

- Programs that recognize the patterns of formal elements that combine to form words, phrases, clauses and textual units (e.g. at2ps).
- Language-specific auxiliary files (e.g. Lexicon, Word Grammar).
- Data sets, built up gradually, containing all patterns registered in the analysis (e.g. Analytical Lexicon)
- Programs that use the data sets and the auxiliary files to make proposals in the interactive procedures for the linguistic analysis (e.g. Analyse).

3.10 Relation with requirements

Some typical features of the workflow serve to meet the requirements defined in section 1.3. The procedure of encoding rather than tagging guarantees consistency in the analysis of morphemes, because the functional deductions are produced automatically. It has the advantage that not only the interpretation of a word, but also the data which led to a certain interpretation can be retrieved, whereas the motivation behind a tagging is usually not visible. It also has the advantage that both the surface forms and the functional analysis are preserved.

By using the language-specific auxiliary files we take our starting-point in the scholarly tradition of Semitic studies, but the encoding system allows us to test alternative interpretations of the data (see below, section 4.5).

4 The verbal paradigm

4.1 Traditional grammars

We will now illuminate our model by taking a look at the verbal paradigm. For the moment we will restrict ourselves to the paradigm of the suffix conjugation. In the traditional grammars we find the following inflection paradigm:

	singular		plural	
3 m	–		*w* – *wn*	[silent] (*un*)
3 f	*t*	(*at*)	– *y*	 [silent]
2 m	*t*	(*t*)	*twn*	(*ton*)
2 f	*ty*	(*t*)	*tyn*	(*ten*)
1 c	*t*	(*et*)	*n* *nn*	(*n*) (*nan*)

Table 2: Paradigm of the perfect in Classical Syriac according to traditional grammars

4.2 Manuscript evidence

Since we work with real manuscripts, we have to deal with the forms that are actually attested. As appears from the paradigm in table 2, for example, the perfect 3mp sometimes has no verbal ending. What is not recorded in the traditional grammars is that there are also forms 3ms with the ending -*w*. This may be due to the fact that the -*w* in the plural, even if it were represented in writing, was not pronounced.[5] Traditionally the singular forms with -*w* are taken as errors, due to the confusion with the silent -*w* in the plural.

The Leiden Peshitta edition takes such readings as 'orthographic variants'. They do not appear in the critical apparatus to the text, but in a separate *Index Orthographicus*. The general preface to the edition contains a long list of categories of orthographical variation (cf. sample 15).

2.2 varietates inflectionis
2.2.1 afformativa
2.2.1.1 perfectum
e.g. 3 msg + *waw*
3 f.sg *yodh*
2 m.sg + *yodh*
2 f.sg *om yodh*
3 m.pl *om waw*
3 f.pl + *waw*
3 f. pl + *yodh*
1 pl cum des -*nan* etc., etc.

Sample 15: Excerpt from General Preface of Leiden Peshitta Edition: categories of *Index Orthographicus*

These categories are referred to in the *Index Orthographicus* of each volume. Thus we find in the text of Song of Songs in the sample edition:

2.2 varietates flectionis:
2.2.1.1. afformativa *perfecti*
2 f. sg + *yodh*
√ ܗܘܐ (I); √ ܪܒܐ (II)
1_7 II 912
8_{10} I 16g6 19 < ?a1

3 f. pl. + *yodh*
√ نفق (I); √ هلك (II)
4_2 II 10m1.3 11m1.2.4-6 13m1 15a2 17a1.2.4.5.10 18h3
5_5 I 13c1 15a2 16g2.3[1].8.9 17a1-8.10.11 17c1(*vid*) 17g2.6 17h2 18c2[1] 18h3 19g5[1].7

Sample 16: Excerpt from *Index Orthographicus* to Song of Songs in sample volume of Leiden Peshitta edition

Unfortunately, the Peshitta project soon abandoned the inclusion of the *Index Orthograhicus*. It appears only in the sample edition and one other volume (Vol. IV/6, containing Odes, the Prayer of Manasseh, Apocryphal Psalms, Psalms of Solomon, Tobit and 1(3) Esdras).

[5] Admittedly, it can be problematic to make claims about the pronunciation on the basis of written sources, but there are strong arguments for this claim, including the fact that the final letter is ignored in punctuation, that it is frequently omitted in writing (Nöldeke, 2001:§50), and that it does not affect poetic patterns (Brockelmann, 1960:45).

4.3 Encoding the attested forms

In the word-level analysis (cf. section 2.1) the forms listed in table 2 are encoded as follows:

	singular	plural
3m	KTB[	KTB[W KTB[(W KTB[W&N
3f	KTB[T==	KTB[(J= KTB[J=
2m	KTB[T=	KTB[TWN
2f	KTB[TJ	KTB[TJN
1c	KTB[T	KTB[N KTB[N&N

Table 3: Encoded forms of Classical Syriac perfect

As we said above, the square bracket to the right marks the verbal ending and the ampersand a paradigmatically unexpected letter. Thus our encoding in table 3 implies that we take the verbal ending *-wn* as an allomorph of *-w* with an additional *-n*. Alternatively we could decide to introduce a separate morpheme *-wn* besides *-w*. The equals sign is used for the disambiguation of forms that have the same consonantal representation. We use it to distinguish the three verbal endings *-t* and for distinguishing the *-y* of the perfect 3fs from the *-y* of the imperative 3fs.

A round bracket marks a paradigmatically expected but absent letter. Thus we have taken the imperfect form 3fs KTBJ as the paradigmatic form, although KTB occurs as well.

4.4 Paradigmatic forms and their realizations

To deal with this material in an appropriate way it is important to use an encoding system in which both the attested surface forms and the abstract morphemes can be retrieved. Thus *'wqdw* 'they burnt (it)' (Judges 1:8; our transcription: >WQDW) is a form of the verb *yqd* (JQD), with the causative prefix *'-* (>). We mark the causative stem morpheme with two square brackets to the left (cf. sample 8), indicate with the round bracket to the right that the first letter of the lexeme is absent, and mark with the ampersand the *w* that has come instead. The square bracket to the right marks the verbal ending. This results in the following encoding:

```
Encoding:             ]>](J&WQD[W
Paradigmatic forms:   >  JQD   W
Realizations:         >  WQD   W
```

4.5 Language variation and language development

This way of encoding the verb forms attested in multiple textual witnesses provides us with a large database from which language variation data can be retrieved. In some cases language development is involved as well, and the data can be used for diachronic analysis. For this research we can build upon the work done by the Syriac scholar Sebastian Brock. One of the phenomena Brock (2003:99–100) observed was that in West Syriac Biblical manuscripts some orthographic innovations are attested, including the addition of a *-y* to the perfect 3fp, the imperfect 3fs and, on analogy, the perfect 3fs. It is a debated issue whether this ending reflects a morpheme that was once pronounced (thus Boyarin, 1981) or just an orthographic convention (thus Brock, 2003; cf. Van Peursen, 2008:244).

4.6 An experiment

Our approach enables us to deploy a practice that is completely new in Syriac scholarship, namely the possibility of testing assumptions upon the data (cf. Talstra & Dyk, 2006). We can test, for example, what happens if we redefine the distribution of *ktb* and *ktbw* (cf. section 4.2) and take the zero ending and the *-w* as allomorphs for the 3rd person masculine.

In our model such a reinterpretation of the material can be registered formally by changing the relevant sections in the Word Grammar. Since the lemmatization is done automatically on the basis of the morphologically encoded text and a functional description of the morphemes, there is no need to change the lemmatization in all separate instances manually.

We have done this experiment for Judges 1 in nineteen manuscripts. This chapter contains 54 perfect forms 3m (except for third-weak verbs). In the bottom-up analysis (cf. section 2) the effect is that the decision on whether a 3m verb is singular or plural is not taken at word level, but at a later stage of the procedure, in which the verb is matched with a subject or another element that reveals its number.

At first sight the results of our experiment were not exciting. In those 26 cases where the grammatical number of the subject is unambiguous, the 'regular' forms are dominant: Only three times is there an irregular form (singular *ktbw* or plural *ktb*), once in one manuscript, twice in two manuscripts.[6] Nevertheless, our experiment yielded some interesting observations.

In the first place we discovered that in 28 cases the grammatical number remained ambiguous even in the clause-level analysis because the subject was a collective noun (which in Syriac can take either a singular or a plural).

In these ambiguous cases the traditional analysis of *ktb* as a singular and *ktbw* as a plural implies a striking alternation of singular and plural forms, e.g. 1:10 'and Judah went (*w'zl*, singular) … and [they] *killed* (*wqṭlw*, plural)'. In our experiment, this became mere orthographic variation. Consequently, in the final stage of the bottom-up analytical procedure, the text hierarchical analysis (section 2.4), we arrived at a more elegant text hierarchical structure, because many of the recurrent subject changes caused by the singular/plural alternation had been resolved.

Secondly, the experiment overcame the rather arbitrary division between 'real' and orthographic variants in the Leiden Peshitta edition. In this edition, whenever there may be some doubt as to whether the verb is in the singular or in the plural, variation between *ktb* and *ktbw* forms is taken as 'real' and the variant is included in the critical apparatus; whenever there is no doubt, the variation is considered orthographic and the variant is listed in the *Index Orthographicus* (sample edition and vol. IV/6) or not mentioned at all (other volumes; cf. Dirksen, 1972:vii-ix).

This editorial policy leads to the somewhat arbitrary decision that *nḥt* 'descended' in 1:9 (Ms 16c1, 16g3; other manuscripts: *nḥtw*) is an orthographic variant, because the subject is the plural *bny yhwd'* 'sons of Judah, Judahites', whereas in 1:10, where the subject is just *yhwd'* 'Judah', *'zlw* 'went' (Ms 17a3; other manuscripts: *'zl*) is a real variant. In 1:26, the same form *'zlw* (Ms 19c1; other manuscripts have again *'zl*) is taken as orthographic, because the subject is the singular noun *gbr'* '(the) man'. In our experiment all these variant readings are treated equally.

5 Conclusions

We hope to have shown how the analytical procedure (section 2) and the workflow of the word-level analysis (section 3) meet the challenges of working with ancient documents (section 1), due to their form-to-function approach, their use of encoding rather than tagging, their distinction between paradigmatic forms and their realizations, and because of the exigencies of accuracy in the case of an ancient limited corpus.

In the word-level analysis we lean heavily on existing grammars. For that reason our approach could be regarded as theory-driven, even though we consider it one of our main tasks to revise and refine the paradigm on the basis of the actual corpora. Our encodings should be considered as hypotheses about the data that can be subjected to testing and experiment (section 4.6).

Unlike projects that concern the acceleration of POS tagging (Ringger *et al.,* 2007; Caroll *et al.*, 2007) we start one level below, with the morphology. 'Encoding rather than tagging' is not just a practical, but a crucial methodological characteristic of our model. (For new insights that it produced regarding Syriac morphology see the publications by Bakker, Van Keulen and Van Peursen in the bibliography). We differ from the computer implementation of morphological rules (Kiraz, 2001) in that our work is more deductive and focused on the interaction between orthography and morphology, because we start with the actual forms attested in the manuscripts. Our position in relation to these other projects is mainly determined by the philological demands that direct our research (see section 1).

Whereas at the morphological level the information provided by traditional grammars is relatively stable, at the higher linguistic levels they provide much less solid ground. The gradually built up datasets (analogous to the Analytical Lexicon at word level) of phrase patterns, clause patterns, or verbal valence contain much information that is not properly dealt with in traditional grammars. At these levels the analysis becomes more data-oriented. Thus in the analysis of phrase structure Van Peursen (2007) found many complex patterns that have not been dealt with in traditional grammars.

We have taken our examples from Syriac, but the same analytical procedures have been applied to other forms of Aramaic (Biblical Aramaic and Targum Aramaic) and Biblical Hebrew. Because of the separation of the analytical programs and the language-specific auxiliary files, it should be possible to apply it to other languages as well. This would mainly require writing the appropriate language definition files. Although our model is in principle language-independent, the morphological analysis presented in this paper is especially apt for Semitic languages because of their rich morphology.

[6] 26 forms × 19 manuscripts = 494 forms in all the manuscripts together. Accordingly, the 5 (1+2×2) irregular forms make up 1%.

Acknowledgments

This paper has benefited much from the valuable input of other members of the project 'Turgama: Computer-Assisted Analysis of the Peshitta and the Targum: Text, Language and Interpretation' of the Leiden Institute for Religious Studies; from the documentation of the *Werkgroep Informatica* of the Vrije Universiteit, Amsterdam; and from the collations of variant readings in the Peshitta manuscripts to Judges by Dr P.B. Dirksen in the archive of the Peshitta Institute Leiden.

References

Bakker, D., 2008. Lemma and Lexeme: The Case of Third-Aleph and Third-Yodh Verbs. Pp. 11–25 in FSL3.

Boyarin, Daniel. 1981. An Inquiry into the Formation of the Middle Aramaic Dialects. Pp. 613–649 in *Bono Homini Donum. Essays in Historical Linguistics in Memory of J. Alexander Kerns*, Vol. II. Edited by Y.L. Arbeitman and A.R. Bomhard. Amsterdam Studies in the Theory and History of Linguistic Science; Series IV: Current Issues in Linguistic History 16. Amsterdam: John Benjamins.

Brock, Sebastian P. 2003. Some Diachronic Features of Classical Syriac. Pp. 95–111 in *Hamlet on a Hill: Semitic and Greek Studies Presented to Professor T. Muraoka on the Occasion of his Sixty-Fifth Birthday*. Edited by M.F.J. Baasten and W.Th. van Peursen. Orientalia Lovaniensia Analecta 118. Leuven: Peeters.

Brockelmann, Carl. 1976. *Syrische Grammatik*. 12th edition. Leipzig: Verlag Enzyklopädie.

Carroll, James L., Robbie Haertel, Peter McClanahan, Eric Ringger, and Kevin Seppi. 2007. Modeling the Annotation Process for Ancient Corpus Creation. in Chatressar 2007, *Proceedings of the International Conference of Electronic Corpora of Ancient Languages (ECAL),* Prague, Czech Republic, November 2007.

Dirksen, P.B. 1972. *The Transmission of the Text of the Book of Judges*. Monographs of the Peshitta Institute Leiden 1. Leiden: Brill.

Dirksen, P.B. 1978. 'Judges', in *The Old Testament in Syriac according to the Peshiṭta Version* Vol. II/2 *Judges, Samuel*. Leiden: Brill.

Dyk, Janet W. and Wido van Peursen. 2008. *Foundations for Syriac Lexicography III. Colloquia of the International Syriac Language Project*. Perspectives on Syriac Linguistics 4; Piscataway, NJ. Gorgias. [= FSL3]

Heal, Kristian S. and Alison Salvesen. Forthcoming. *Foundations for Syriac Lexicography IV. Colloquia of the International Syriac Language Project*. Perspectives on Syriac Linguistics 5. Piscataway, NJ: Gorgias. [= FSL4]

Keulen, P.S.F. van, 2008. Feminine Nominal Endings in Hebrew, Aramaic and Syriac: Derivation or Inflection? Pp. 27–39 in FSL3.

Keulen, P.S.F. van and W.Th. van Peursen. 2006. *Corpus Linguistics and Textual History. A Computer-Assisted Interdisciplinary Approach to the Peshitta*. Studia Semitica Neerlandica 48. Assen: Van Gorcum.

Kiraz, George Anton. 2001. *Computational Nonlinear Morphology. With Emphasis on Semitic Languages*. Studies in Natural Language Processing. Cambridge: Cambridge University Press.

Nöldeke, Theodor. 2001. *Compendious Syriac Grammar*. Translated from the second improved German edition by J.A. Crichton. Winona Lake: Eisenbrauns.

Peursen, W.Th. van and Bakker, D. Forthcoming. Lemmatization and Grammatical Categorization: The Case of ܗܟܢ in Classical Syriac. In FSL4

Peursen, W.Th. van. 2008. Inflectional Morpheme or Part of the Lexeme: Some Reflections on the Shaphel in Classical Syriac. Pp. 41–57 in FSL3.

Peursen, W.Th. van. 2007. *Language and Interpretation in the Syriac Text of Ben Sira. A Comparative Linguistic and Literary Study*. Monographs of the Peshitta Institute Leiden 16. Leiden: Brill.

Peursen, W.Th. van. 2008. Language Variation, Language Development and the Textual History of the Peshitta. Pp. 231–256 in *Aramaic in its Historical and Linguistic Setting*. Edited by H. Gzella and M.L. Folmer. Veröffentlichungen der Orientalischen Kommission 50. Wiesbaden: Harrassowitz.

Peursen, W.Th. van. Forthcoming. Numerals and Nominal Inflection in Classical Syriac. In FSL4.

Ringger, Eric, Peter McClanahan, Robbie Haertel, George Busby, Marc Carmen, James Carroll, Kevin Seppi and Deryle Lonsdale. 2007. Active Learning for Part-of-Speech Tagging: Accelerating Corpus Annotation. Pp. 101–108 in *Proceedings of the ACL Linguistic Annotation Workshop, Association for Computational Linguistics*. Prague, Czech Republic, June 2007.

Sikkel, Constantijn J. 2008. Lexeme Status of Pronominal Suffixes. Pp. 59–67 in FSL3.

Talstra, Eep, and Dyk, Janet W. 2006. The Computer and Biblical Research: Are there Perspectives beyond the Imitation of Classical Instruments? Pp. 189–203 in *Text, Translation, and Tradition*. Edited by W.Th. van Peursen and R.B. ter Haar Romeny. Monographs of the Peshitta Institute Leiden 14. Leiden: Brill.

The Karamel System and Semitic Languages: Structured Multi-Tiered Morphology

François Barthélemy
CNAM-Cedric, Paris, France
INRIA-Alpage, Rocquencourt, France
francois.barthelemy@cnam.fr

Abstract

Karamel is a system for finite-state morphology which is multi-tape and uses a typed Cartesian product to relate tapes in a structured way. It implements statically compiled feature structures. Its language allows the use of regular expressions and Generalized Restriction rules to define multi-tape transducers. Both simultaneous and successive application of local constraints are possible. This system is interesting for describing rich and structured morphologies such as the morphology of Semitic languages.

1 Introduction

Karamel is a system for defining and executing multi-tape finite-state transducers where relationships between tapes are expressed using a tree structure. This structure is obtained through embedded units, which are used to analyze a tuple of strings recognized by the transducer. For instance, the units considered in an example may be affix, form and sentence.

The system includes a language and an Integrated Development Environment. The language uses extended regular expressions, computations and contextual rules. The environment provides a graphical interface to write and execute finite-state descriptions.

Karamel has many applications. For Natural Language Processing, it may be used for morphological analysis, transliteration, parsing, etc. This paper is dedicated to the application of Karamel to the morphological analysis of Semitic languages, for which both multiple tapes and complex structures are useful.

Some descriptions of the morphology of Semitic Languages use several tiers. For instance, (McCarthy, 1981) uses four tiers, one for prefixes, one for the root, one for the template (consonant-vowel pattern) and the last one for the vocalization.

Such a multi-tiered description may be implemented using a cascade of 2-tape machines (Beesley, 1998) or using a multi-tape transducer where each tier is described by a tape and the surface form by an additional tape. This is the approach of G. A. Kiraz for the Syriac language (Kiraz, 2000). Karamel is designed for the later solution.

The multi-tape feature is also interesting for describing related dialects, whenever a great part of the analysis may be shared. A separate tape is dedicated to the surface form in each dialect.

The Semitic Morphology is strongly structured by the roots. The basis of an analysis is the identification of the root. Furthermore, several layers of affixes may be distinguished around the core containing the roots: paradigmatic prefixes; affixes encoding the person, gender and number; clitics such as pronouns. This structure is conveniently defined using Karamel's units.

In the following section of the paper, we present Karamel's language, its theoretical background and its syntax. Section 3 describe the other aspects of the Karamel System: its development environment, its current state and future evolutions. Then comes an example of Semitic morphology written in Karamel, the description of Akkadian verbal flexion. The last section compares Karamel to some other systems.

2 The Karamel language

The language is based on a subclass of rational n-ary relations called *multi-grain relations* which is closed under intersection and difference (Barthélemy, 2007b). They are defined using rational expressions extended with a typed Cartesian product. This operator implements the notion of unit used to give a tree-structure to tuples of the

Proceedings of the EACL 2009 Workshop on Computational Approaches to Semitic Languages, pages 10–18,
Athens, Greece, 31 March, 2009.

relations. A unit is an inner-node of the structure.

A project is a set of finite-state machine defined over the same universe: the same alphabet, the same tape set, the same units. A project begins with declarations defining this universe. It continues with an ordered sequence of machine definitions.

The declaration section contains several clauses including classes, tapes and unit definitions. A class of symbols is a finite set of symbols. Here are some examples of class definitions:

```
class short_v is a, e, i, u;
class long_v is aa, ee, ii, uu;
class vow is a, e, i, u, long_v;
```

A symbol may belong to several classes. In the definition of a class, another class name may appear and is just an abbreviation for all its members. The class names are also used in regular expressions to denote the disjunction of their members.

The symbols written using several letters and/or digits, when there is a risk of confusion with a string of symbols, must be written enclosed by < and >. For instance, the long a is written `aa` in the class definition (`long_v`) but in a regular expression, it must be written `<aa>` because `aa` denotes a string of two short vowels. The bracketing with < and > is also used for special characters such as the space < >, punctuation marks (e.g. <,>) and the empty string <>.

A tape is declared with its name and the alphabet of the symbols which may appear on it.

```
tape dig: <digit>,
     fr, en: <letter>|< >|<->;
```

The alphabet is defined using a regular expression made with symbols, classes and length-preserving operators such as the disjunction and the difference.

A Karamel unit is a typed Cartesian product. The type consists in i) a number of components and ii) the tapes contained by each component. In the declaration, there is also a default value for each component.

```
unit seg is {d: dig = <digit>*;
             f: fr = <letter>*;
             e: en = <letter>*}
unit num is
        {c: dig, fr, en={seg}+}
```

The unit `seg` (for *segment*) contains three components, each using a single tape. The unit `num` (for *number*) has one component which contains three tapes (`dig, fr` and `en`).

The default value is a non-empty sequence of units of type `seg`. Cartesian products are written in regular expressions as tuples with the type name followed by the components: `{seg: 2(0?),vingt,twenty}`. Component names may be used instead of their position `{seg:e=twenty,f=vingt,d=2(0?)}`. When a component is omitted, the default value is implied. The notation `{seg}` (cf. the default value of the component `c` in `num`) is a unit `seg` with default values in all the components. Units may be embedded:

```
{num:{seg:2,vingt,twenty}
     {seg:2,-deux,-two}}
```

This example is a structured representation of the triplet `(22,vingt-deux,twenty-two)`.

In Karamel, there are three ways of defining a finite-state transducer: by a regular expression, by a computation or by a contextual rule. Regular expressions use symbols, classes of symbols, rational operations and standard extensions (for instance, optionality written ?). Furthermore, intersection, difference and negation are also available although these operations are usually not defined on transducers.

Regular expressions are defined using the `regexp` construction:

```
regexp zero is
  {seg: 0,zéro,(zero|naught)};
  {seg: <digit>*-0};
end
```

A *regexp* contains a non empty sequence of regular expressions ended with a semicolon. It denotes the disjunction of these expressions.

The second way of defining a machine is by applying operators to already defined machines. All the operators used in regular expressions may appear in such a computation, but there are some other operators as well. The first one is the *projection* which removes one or several tapes from its operand. The second one is the *external product* which combines a n-ary relation with a language on a given tape. It is used to *apply* a transducer to a given input which is not split in units yet. All possible partitioning of the input in units is first computed, and then it is intersected with one tape of the transducer. The reverse operation is the external projection which extracts a language from a relation on a given tape by first applying the simple projection and then removing unit boundaries. These two operations are used to transduce a given possibly non-deterministic input into an output.

```
let segments=
      union(star(non_zero),zero);
```

The *let* is followed by an expression in prefixed notation with the operators written with letters. The literals are the names of previously defined machine. In our example, the expression uses the machines `zero` defined by the previous `regexp` and `non_zero` (not given here).

The last way for defining a machine consists in the Generalized Restriction Rules defined in (Yli-Jyrä and Koskenniemi, 2004). Roughly speaking, these rules are a modernized version of classical Two-Level Rules such as Context Restriction and Surface Coercion rules (Koskenniemi, 1983). They also are comparable to the rewrite rules of Xerox Finite-State Tools (Beesley and Karttunen, 2003), the difference being that rewrite rules are applied in cascades whereas GR rules may be simultaneous.

Contextual rules are defined using three regular expressions:

```
gr_rule rzero is
  {num}
constraint
    {num:seg={seg}*{seg:#0}{seg}*}
=> {num:seg={seg:#0,zéro}}
end
```

The first expression defines a universe. All the expressions in the universe which match the pattern on the left of the arrow must also match the pattern on the right. The sharp symbol is an auxiliary symbol used to make sure that the 0 on both sides is the same occurrence of this symbol. It identifies the *center* of the contextual rule. For more details about the semantics of Generalized Restriction rules, see (Yli-Jyrä and Koskenniemi, 2004).

Karamel implements non-recursive feature structures. Feature values are ordinary symbols and feature structures are typed. The types must be declared in the declaration section of the description. Feature Structures may appear anywhere in regular expressions. They are usually put on one or several specific tapes. They are statically compiled. Feature Structures are to be used with caution, because they allow the expression of long-distance dependencies which are costly and may lead to a combinatorial explosion. The feature structure compilation techniques come from (Barthélemy, 2007a).

A type is defined as follows:

```
fstruct Name is
     [gen=gender,num=1|2|3]
```

where `gender` is a class and 1, 2, 3 are symbols. Each feature is defined with its name and its domain of values, which is a finite set of symbols defined by a regular expression. A feature structure of this type is written as follows: `[Name:gen=masc,num=2]`. As usual, it is possible to specify only part of the features and their order is not important. The type name at the beginning is mandatory. Feature structures are compiled using auxiliary symbols which are not known by the user. The type name denotes a class of symbols containing all the symbols which may be used to compile a structure of this type, including auxiliary symbols.

Regular expressions and contextual rules may use variables which take their values in finite set of symbols. An expression with such a variable stands for the disjunction of all the possible valuation of the variables. Variables are especially useful to express feature structure unification.

The language offers macros called *abbreviations*. An abbreviation is a notation for an already declared unit where part of the components is defined in the declaration and another part is defined in the call. Here is an example.

```
abbrev teen is {d: dig = <digit>;
               f: fr =<letter>*;
              e: en = <letter>*}
  for {seg: 1 @d, @f,@e teen}
```

In an expression, `{teen: 6, seize,six}` is expanded in `{seg: 16,seize,sixteen}` before the compilation.

3 The Karamel System

The core of the system consists in a compiler written in Python which compiles Karamel descriptions into finite-state automata which are interpreted as transducers by the system. The compiler uses the *FSM* and *Lextools* toolkits by AT&T Research. A Karamel regular expression is first compiled in the Lextools format, then the Lextools compiler is called to compile it in FSM binary format. Some Karamel operations over transducers such as the intersection, the union, the concatenation are directly implemented by the corresponding FSM operation on automata. Some other operations such as the two projections and the external product are performed by a script calling a sequence of FSM computations.

The development environment uses a Graphical User Interface written in HTML, CSS and Javascript. There are three main subparts: project management (creation, deletion, import, export, duplication); project development: creation, deletion, renaming, reordering, checking, compilation of a machine; machine execution, with optional introduction of run-time input, filtering of the result, projection on one or several tapes.

A dependency graph is maintained in order to ensure that a change in one machine is taken into account in all the machines which depend on it. For instance if there is the following definition: `let m3=union(m1,m2);`, any change in m_1 implies a recompilation of m_3. This recompilation is not necessarily immediate. A status is associated to each machine. The change in m_1 results in a change in the statuses of m_1 and m_3.

At the moment, the execution of a machine is possible only through the GUI, using a browser. The development of a C++ or Python function to interpret the FSM machine with the Karamel semantics is not a difficult task, but it is still to be done. Another weakness of the current version of the system is the type-checking which is not fully implemented. The type system is simple and the language is strongly typed, so every type error should be found at compile time. It is not the case yet.

Karamel will be distributed to a few kind betatesters in a near future. We plan to add some test facilities to the environment. At medium term, a migration from FSM to openFST (Allauzen et al., 2007) and a distribution under the LGPL license are envisaged.

So far, Karamel has been used for morphology. A morphological analyzer for the Akkadian verb is presented in the next section. It is a medium size grammar. Another project describes the French morphology. It is the translation in Karamel of a grammar developed for the MMORPH system (Petitpierre and Russel, 1995). The grammar has a large coverage. It has been tested with a toy lexicon only. The other domain of application explored so far is the transliteration domain. There is a multilingual description of numbers that relates the notation with digits to a written form in several languages (French, English, Finnish). A tape is devoted to each language, a tape to the digits and several tapes for feature structures, some of which are language specific. Another project transliterates Egyptian hieroglyphs into the Latin alphabet, using an intermediate representation on a third tape.

4 An example: the Akkadian verb

In this section, we present an application of Karamel to Semitic morphology, namely a description of Akkadian verbal forms.

Akkadian is the language of the ancient Mesopotamia. It was written in cuneiform, from around 2500 B.C. up to the first century B.C. It is the main representative of the eastern branch of Semitic languages. It is divided in seven main dialects with many local variations. Its verbal morphology is a typical semitic one, with a great number of triliteral roots, some stems with usual flexion (prefixation, reduplication, infixation, vocalization). There are two infixes, `t` and `tn`. Their presence is almost orthogonal with the presence of a stem prefix and the reduplication of the second radical.

The description of the morphology in Karamel is based on a two-level structure. The first level separates verbal forms in three layers:

- a core, which contains the root, its vocalization, and also the prefixes which depend on the stem and/or aspect, infixes and gemination.
- personal affixes (prefixes and suffixes), which encode the person, the number, the gender and the case (when relevant).
- the clitics: enclitic pronoun and proclitic particles.

In the following, these units will be called *big grains*.

The second level is used for the core only, which is divided in smaller parts using the two following criteria: firstly, a unit must be significant in the analysis; secondly, it is determined by a set of features in such a way that no smaller part is uniquely determined by a subset of these features and no greater part is determined by the same set of features. Such a component is invariable for a given value of its features, except some surface transformations.

Following the proposition of (Malbran-Labat, 2001), three kinds of vowels are distinguished. The first kind of vowel depends on the stem and the aspect. They are called *aspectual vowels*. The second kind, called *lexical vowel* depends on the stem, the aspect and a lexical category attached to the root. The third kind of vowels, the *support vowels* are not related to morphological features. They are necessary to pronounce and/or write[1] the form. The first two kinds of vowels are systematically preserved in weak forms whereas support vowels disappear in weak consonant neighborhood. Support vowel are member of the small grain containing the preceding consonant whereas lexical and aspectual vowels constitute small grains.

The different subparts of the core and their features are given in figure 1. They will be called *small grains*.

The figure 2 gives some extracts of the project. It begins with the declaration section. There is a class of all letters, subclasses of consonants, weak consonants, strong consonants, vowels, long vowels, short vowels. There is also a class for each feature domain. Several types of feature structures are defined: one for each kind of big grain (core, personal affix, pronoun, enclitic particle); a unique type for all the kinds of small grains.

The description has five tapes. The first tape contains the feature structures associated with big grains, the second tape contains the feature structures covering small grains. The third tape contains a canonical form of each grain. It correspond to the *lexical form* of traditional Two-Level grammars. The last two tapes contain the surface forms respectively in the Babylonian and the Assyrian dialects, which are slightly different, mostly in their vocalization.

Here is an example of structured analysis of the form *iptarasū*.

pers pref	core					pers suff
	rad 1	stem infix	rad 2	lex vowel	rad 3	
i	p	ta	r	a	s	ū

The tape scheme does not correspond to a multi-tiered analysis. There are several reasons for this. The first one comes from the Akkadian language. The stems and aspects are not described by patterns but divided in smaller analysis units, in particular stem analysis uses the two orthogonal dimensions called here *stem1* and *stem2*: the first one notes stem gemination and prefixation and the later, infixation. A stem is a pair (stem1,stem2). The vocalization does not require patterns of two vowels separated by the middle radical, but in most cases a pattern of only one vowel.

Another reason comes from the Karamel language: the information usually encoded in tiers appears in the unit types. For instance the information about the root tier appears in small grains of type *radical*. Similarly, the vocalization appears in the small grains of types *aspect vowel* and *lexical vowel*. The rich tree structure is sufficient to express clearly the analysis.

The morphotactics of the language is described as the sum of local constraints. It involves only the first three tapes. The elementary units, namely small grains and all the big grains but the core, are described separately. For instance, the machine `aspect_infix` (cf. figure 2) distinguishes two cases: if the feature `aspect` has `perfect` as value, then there is a small grain of type `ifx_parf` containing the infix `ta`; if the feature `aspect` has another value, then there is no grain of type `ifx_parf` in the core. The two cases are given using two different regular expressions. For more complex small grains, more cases are to be described, up to 13 for the lexical vowels which have different colors and length depending on 4 features.

Two finite-state machines describe the order of respectively small and big grains. The one for small grains called `core_morphotactics` is sketched in the figure.

The lexicon is given using a macro called `lexent`. A `lexent` (for *lexical entry*) tuple looks like a usual lexicon entry, with only lexical information, although it is a regular expression denoting a complete core, with its prefix, infixes, vowels, etc. The `lexicon` finite state machine may be directly intersected with the `sg_order` machine previously defined and all the other constraints in order to obtain a machine describing all the possible cores build on the roots given in the lexicon.

The computation of the two surface forms for

[1] The cuneiform writing is syllabic. It is impossible to write a consonant without a vowel immediately before or after it.

subpart	stem1	stem2	aspect	class	root	example
aspect prefix	X	X	X			**mu**parrisu
stem prefix	X					**šu**prusu
radical					X	ip**r**us
core infix		X				ip**ta**ras
stem1 gemination	X					upa**rr**as
aspect gemination	X	X	X			ipa**rr**as
aspect vowel	X	X	X			uparr**i**s
lexical vowel	X	X	X	X		ipr**u**s

Figure 1: Subparts and features

the two dialects is performed by a set of constraints written using regular expressions and contextual rules. They relate the lexical form and one or both surface forms. The features are used in some of them.

Rules are used for phenomena which may occur several times in a given form. For instance, the deletion of support vowels before another vowel may appear in several places: before lexical and aspectual vowels, but also when a weak consonant disappears or changes to a vowel.

In many cases however, surface transformation occur only in one given place of a form and the use of a rule is not necessary. The tree structure helps in characterizing this place. The example given in the figure is the coloration of the first vowel in some stems (II and III).

The grammar presently covers strong forms, 1-weak verbs and part of 2-weak and 3-weak verbs. Verbs with two or three weak consonants[2] and quadriliteral roots are not covered at all. The description uses 27 `regexp` clauses, 22 `let` and 6 rules.

4.1 Comparisons with other systems

There are many systems for writing finite-state machines. In this section we compare Karamel with some of them which are specialized in morphological descriptions.

The most popular system is probably the Xerox Finite State Tool (Beesley and Karttunen, 2003). It has been used, among others, for the description of Arabic morphology (Beesley, 1998). The interdigitation is handled using a compile-replace process using the replace operator (Karttunen and Beesley, 2000) (Karttunen, 1995).

The computational model is a sequential one, where two-tape transducers are merged using the *composition* operation. The descriptions are oriented, with an input and an output, but the transduction has not to be deterministic and the machines are invertible. The strings are not structured, but some structure may be marked using auxiliary symbols inserted when necessary by the user.

In order to fulfill the constraints that there are only two tapes, grammars often put heterogeneous data on a tape. For instance, the features and the lexical representations are put together on the input tape. Intermediate forms in the cascade often contain a mix of lexical and surface representations.

There are no feature structures in XFST, but features written as ordinary symbols. The scope and the unifications are written by the user.

Karamel is more declarative than XFST. Information of different natures are put on different tapes. Abstract feature structures are available. Their compilation and the unifications are automated. On the other hand, XFST is more efficient. The structure information is put only where necessary.

XFST is distributed under a commercial license.

The system MAGEAD is another system of finite-state morphology developed for Arabic dialects (Habash and Rambow, 2006). It follows the multi-tape approach proposed by George Anton Kiraz for the Syriac language (Kiraz, 2000). It has a rule-based language following the principles of (Grimley-Evans et al., 1996) in which a notion of *partition* splits forms in a sequence of units comparable to Karamel's units. But in this approach, there is only one kind of unit which relates all the tapes. Like Karamel, MAGEAD is a layer above Lextools and FSM. The system is not distributed and its description in published papers is not very detailed.

[2] There is a Akkadian verb with 3 weak consonants as root.

Declarations

```
class vowel is a, e, i, u, aa, ee, ii, uu;
class cons is b, d, g, h, ...
class num is sing, dual, plur;
class aspect is present, preterit, perfect, ...
...
fstruct fspers is [asp=aspect,pers=pers,num=num,gen=gen]
fstruct fscore is [stem1=stem1,stem2=stem2,asp=aspect,lex=lex]
...
tape lex: letter, bab: letter, assy: letter, sg: fssg,
     bg :  fspers|fscore|fsclit;
unit sgrain is {sg: sg = [fssg]; lex: lex = <letter>*,
                 bab: bab =<letter>*, assy: assy = <letter>*}
unit core is {bg: bg = [fscore];
               smallg: sg, lex, bab, assy = {sgrain}* }
...
abbrev sgi is {r1: bg = [fscore]; r2: sg = [fssg];
                r3: lex = <letter>*}
  for {core: @r1, {sgrain}* {sgrain: @r2, @r3} {sgrain}* }
abbrev lexent is {cfs: bg = [fscore]; fst: lex = <cons>;
                  snd: lex = <cons>; thd: lex = <cons>}
  for {core: @cfs, {sgrain: [fssg:typ=typ-rad]}*
        {sgrain: [fssg:typ=rad], @fst} {sgrain: [fssg:typ=typ-rad]}*
        {sgrain: [fssg:typ=rad], @snd} {sgrain: [fssg:typ=typ-rad]}*
        {sgrain: [fssg:typ=rad], @thd} }
```

Small grains morphotactics

```
regexp aspect_infix is
  {sgi: [fscore:asp=perfect],[fssg:typ=ifx_parf], ta};
  {core: [fscore:asp=aspect-perfect],
                {sgrain: [fssg:typ=typ-ifx_parf]}* };
end
...
regexp small_grain_order is
  {core: smallg=
    {sgrain: [fssg:typ=asp_pref]}? {sgrain: [fssg:typ=rad]}
    {sgrain: [fssg:typ=ifx_parf]}? {sgrain: [fssg:typ=ifx_parf]}?
    ...
let core_morphotactics=intersect(aspect_infix,stem_gemination,
                                 ...,small_grain_order);
regexp lexicon is
  {lexent: [fscore:lex=a_u,stem1=I|II|IV],p,r,s};
  {lexent: [fscore:lex=a,stem1=I|III],ṣ,b,t};
  ...
let actual_cores=intersect(core_morphotactics,lexicon);
```

Figure 2: extracts from the Akkadian project

Surface transformations

```
gr_rule delete_support_vowels is
   {core}
constraint
   {core: smallg= {sgrain}*
                    #{sgrain: lex=<letter>+<vowel>,bab=<letter><cons>}
                    {sgrain}* }
=>
   {core: smallg= {sgrain}* #{sgrain}
         {sgrain: bab=<>}? {sgrain: lex=<vowel>} {sgrain}*}
end
regexp color_u is
  {core: [fscore:stem1=II|III],
          {sgrain:lex=<cons>?<vowel>,bab=<cons>?u}{sgrain}*};
  {core: [fscore:stem1=I|IV],
          {sgrain:lex=<cons>?<vowel>,bab=<cons>?(<vowel>-u)}
          {sgrain}*};
end
```

Figure 3: extracts from the Akkadian project

The main difference is that MAGEAD has only one level of structure using only one type of Cartesian Products. Another difference is that the two systems use different kinds of contextual rules. The rules differ both by their syntax and their semantics. Furthermore, contextual rules are the main syntactic construction in MAGEAD whereas Karamel uses also regular expressions.

MMORPH is another system of partition-based morphology based on the work by Pulman and Hepple (Pulman and Hepple, 1993). There are two parts in a description: first, the morphotactics is described using a Unification Grammar where the terminals are lexical affixes and the non-terminals are feature structures; transformation rules relate the lexical and surface levels. The features are flat. Feature structures are evaluated dynamically by a unification machine.

Karamel statically compiles Feature Structures and their unification into finite-state transducers. This is efficient and part of the structures are shared. On the other hand, the grammar of feature structures must be regular and there is a risk of combinatorial explosion. MMORPH uses two kinds of units: one relates affixes to Feature Structures, the other relates small parts of lexical and surface forms (typically, substrings of length 0 to 2). Karamel uses a richer and more flexible structuration. Furthermore, the number of tapes is fixed in MMORPH and user defined in Karamel. MMORPH is distributed under the GPL license. It is not maintained any more.

5 Conclusion

In this paper, we have emphasized the application of Karamel to morphological descriptions. The multiplicity of tapes is useful at all the levels of the analysis. The abstract representation typically uses feature structures. Several tapes are to be used if different kinds of feature structures have different spans with respect to the surface form. At the intermediate level, several tapes may be used by a multi-tiered analysis. It is not the case in our example, but Karamel is compatible with an approach where each tier is put on a different tape (Kiraz, 2000). The surface level may also use several tapes. In our example, two tapes are used for two different dialects. It is also possible to use several tapes for several writings of the surface forms, for instance, a standard written form, a phonetic representation using the International Phonetic Alphabet (IPA) and a transcription in Latin alphabet.

The other main feature of Karamel is to use embedded units to relate the different tapes. This is useful to define the scope of feature structure and to distinguish several parts in the forms.

References

Cyril Allauzen, Michael Riley, Johan Schalkwyk, Wojciech Skut, and Mehryar Mohri. 2007. Openfst: A general and efficient weighted finite-state transducer library. In *Implementation and Application of Automata, 12th International Conference, CIAA*, volume 4783 of *LNC*, pages 11–23, Prague, Czech Republic.

François Barthélemy. 2007a. Finite-state compilation of feature structures for two-level morphology. In *International Workshop on Finite State Methods in Natural Language Processing (FSMNLP)*, Potsdam, Germany.

François Barthélemy. 2007b. Multi-grain relations. In *Implementation and Application of Automata, 12th International Conference (CIAA)*, pages 243–252, Prague, Czech Republic.

Kenneth R. Beesley and Lauri Karttunen. 2003. *Finite State Morphology*. CSLI Publications.

Kenneth R. Beesley. 1998. Arabic morphology using only finite-state operations.

Edmund Grimley-Evans, George Kiraz, and Stephen Pulman. 1996. Compiling a partition-based two-level formalism. In *COLING*, pages 454–459, Copenhagen, Denmark.

Nizar Habash and Owen Rambow. 2006. Magead: a morphological analyzer and generator for the Arabic dialects. In *ACL: Proceedings of the 21st International Conference on Computational Linguistics and the 44th annual meeting of the Association for Computational Linguistics*, pages 681–688.

Lauri Karttunen and Kenneth R. Beesley. 2000. Finite-state non-concatenative morphotactics. In *Fifth Workshop of the ACL Special Interest Group in Computational Phonology*, pages 1–12, Luxembourg (Luxembourg).

Lauri Karttunen. 1995. The replace operator. In *ACL-95*, pages 16–23, Boston, Massachusetts. Association for Computational Linguistics.

George Anton Kiraz. 2000. Multitiered nonlinear morphology using multitape finite automata: a case study on Syriac and Arabic. *Comput. Linguist.*, 26(1):77–105.

Kimmo Koskenniemi. 1983. Two-level model for morphological analysis. In *IJCAI-83*, pages 683–685, Karlsruhe, Germany.

Florence Malbran-Labat. 2001. *Manuel de langue akkadienne*. Publications de l'institut Orientaliste de Louvain (50), Peeters.

John J. McCarthy. 1981. A prosodic theory of nonconcatenative morphology. *Linguistic Inquiry*, 12:373–418.

D. Petitpierre and G. Russel. 1995. Mmorph: the multex morphology program. Technical report, ISSCO technical report, Geneva, Switzerland.

S. Pulman and M. Hepple. 1993. A feature-based formalism for two-level phonology. *Computer Speech and Language*, 7.

Anssi Mikael Yli-Jyrä and Kimmo Koskenniemi. 2004. Compiling contextual restrictions on strings into finite-state automata. In *Proceedings of the Eindhoven FASTAR Days 2004 (September 3–4)*, Eindhoven, The Netherlands, December.

Revisiting multi-tape automata for Semitic morphological analysis and generation

Mans Hulden
University of Arizona
Department of Linguistics
`mhulden@email.arizona.edu`

Abstract

Various methods have been devised to produce morphological analyzers and generators for Semitic languages, ranging from methods based on widely used finite-state technologies to very specific solutions designed for a specific language or problem. Since the earliest proposals of how to adopt the elsewhere successful finite-state methods to root-and-pattern morphologies, the solution of encoding Semitic grammars using multi-tape automata has resurfaced on a regular basis. Multi-tape automata, however, require specific algorithms and reimplementation of finite-state operators across the board, and hence such technology has not been readily available to linguists. This paper, using an actual Arabic grammar as a case study, describes an approach to encoding multi-tape automata on a single tape that can be implemented using any standard finite-automaton toolkit.

1 Introduction

1.1 Root-and-pattern morphology and finite-state systems

The special problems and challenges embodied by Semitic languages have been recognized from the early days of applying finite-state methods to natural language morphological analysis. The language model which finite-state methods have been most successful in describing—a model where morphemes concatenate in mostly strict linear order—does not translate congenially to the type of root-and-pattern morphology found in e.g. Arabic and Hebrew (Kataja and Koskenniemi, 1988; Lavie et al., 1988).

In Arabic, as in most Semitic languages, verbs have for a long time been analyzed as consisting of three elements: a (most often) triconsonantal root, such as *ktb* (ك ت ب), a vowel pattern containing grammatical information such as voice (e.g. the vowel *a*) and a derivational template, such as `CVCVC` indicating the class of the verb, all of which are interdigitated to build a stem, such as *katab* (كَتَب).[1] This stem is in turn subject to more familiar morphological constructions including prefixation and suffixation, yielding information such as number, person, etc, such as *kataba* (كَتَبَ), the third person singular masculine perfect form.

The difficulty of capturing this interdigitation process is not an inherent shortcoming of finite-state automata or transducers per se, but rather a result of the methods that are commonly used to construct automata. Regular expressions that contain operations such as concatenation, union, intersection, as well as morphotactic descriptions through right-linear grammars offer an unwieldy functionality when it comes to interleaving strings with one another in a regulated way. But, one could argue, since large scale morphological analyzers as finite-state automata/transducers have indeed been built (see e.g. Beesley (1996, 1998b,a)), the question of how to do it becomes one of construction, not feasibility.

1.2 Multitape automata

One early approach, suggested by Kay (1987) and later pursued in different variants by Kiraz (1994, 2000) among others, was to, instead of modeling morphology along the more traditional finite-state transducer, modeling it with a n-tape automaton, where tapes would carry precisely this interleaving

[1] Following autosegmental analyses, this paper assumes the model where the vocalization is not merged with the pattern, i.e. we do not list separate patterns for vocalizations such as `CaCaC` as is assumed more traditionally. Which analysis to choose largely a matter of convenience, and the methods in this paper apply to either one.

Proceedings of the EACL 2009 Workshop on Computational Approaches to Semitic Languages, pages 19–26,
Athens, Greece, 31 March, 2009.

that is called for in Semitic interdigitation. However, large-scale multitape solutions containing the magnitude of information in standard Arabic dictionaries such as Wehr (1979) have not been reported.

To our knowledge, two large-scale morphological analyzers for Arabic that strive for reasonable completeness have been been built: one by Xerox and one by Tim Buckwalter (Buckwalter, 2004). The Xerox analyzer relies on complex extensions to the finite-state calculus of one and two-tape automata (transducers) as documented in Beesley and Karttunen (2003), while Buckwalter's system is a procedural approach written in Perl which decomposes a word and simultaneously consults lexica for constraining the possible decompositions. Also, in a similar vein to Xerox's Arabic analyzer, Yona and Wintner (2008) report on a large-scale system for Hebrew built on transducer technology. Most importantly, none of these very large systems are built around multi-tape automata even though such a construction from a linguistic perspective would appear to be a fitting choice when dealing with root-and-pattern morphology.

1.3 n-tape space complexity

There is a fundamental space complexity problem with multi-tape automata, which is that when the number of tapes grows, the required joint symbol alphabet grows with exponential rapidity unless special mechanisms are devised to curtail this growth. This explosion in the number of transitions in an n-tape automaton can in many cases be more severe than the growth in the number of states of a complex grammar.

To take a simple, though admittedly slightly artificial example: suppose we have a 5-tape automaton, each tape consisting of the same alphabet of, say 22 symbols $\{s_1, \ldots, s_{22}\}$. Now, assume we want to restrict the co-occurrence of s_1 on any combination of tapes, meaning s_1 can only occur once on one tape in the same position, i.e. we would be accepting any strings containing a symbol such as $s_1{:}s_2{:}s_2{:}s_2{:}s_2$ or $s_2{:}s_2{:}s_2{:}s_2{:}s_3$ but not, $s_1{:}s_2{:}s_3{:}s_4{:}s_1$. Without further treatment of the alphabet behavior, this yields a multi-tape automaton which has a single state, but 5,056,506 transitions—each transition naturally representing a legal combination of symbols on the five tapes. This kind of transition blow-up is not completely inevitable: of course one can devise many tricks to avoid it, such as adding certain semantics to the transition notation—in our example by perhaps having a special type of 'failure' transition which leads to non-acceptance. For the above example this would cut down the number of transitions from 5,056,506 to 97,126. The drawback with such methods is that any changes will tend to affect the entire finite-state system one is working with, requiring adaptations in almost every underlying algorithm to construct automata. One is then unable to leverage the power of existing software designed for finite-state morphological analysis, but needs to build special-purpose software for whatever multi-tape implementation one has in mind.[2]

1.4 The appeal of the multi-tape solution

The reason multi-tape descriptions of natural language morphology are appealing lies not only in that such solutions seem to be able to handle Semitic verbal interdigitation, but also in that a multi-tape solution allows for a natural *alignment* of information regarding segments and their grammatical features, something which is often missing in finite-state-based solutions to morphological analysis. In the now-classical way of constructing morphological analyzers, we have a transducer that maps a string representing an unanalyzed word form, such as *kataba* (كَتَبَ) to a string representing an analyzed one, e.g. `ktb +FormI +Perfect +Act +3P +Masc +Sg`. Such transductions seldom provide grammatical component-wise alignment information telling which parts of the unanalyzed words contribute to which parts of the grammatical information. Particularly if morphemes signifying a grammatical category are discontinuous, this information is difficult to provide naturally in a finite-automaton based system without many tapes. A multi-tape solution, on the other hand,

[2]Two anonymous reviewers point out the work by Habash et al. (2005) and Habash and Rambow (2006) who report an effort to analyze Arabic with such a multitape system based on work by Kiraz (2000, 2001) that relies on custom algorithms devised for a multitape alphabet. Although Habash and Rambow do not discuss the space requirements in their system, it is to be suspected that the number of transitions grows quickly using such an method by virtue of the argument given above. These approaches also use a small number of tapes (between 3 and 5), and, since the number of transitions can increase exponentially with the number of tapes used, such systems do not on the face of it appear to scale well to more than a handful of tapes without special precautions.

T_{input}	k	a	t	a	b	a
T_{root}	k		t		b	
T_{form}	**Form I**					
T_{ptrn}	C	V	C	V	C	
T_{paff}						a
T_{affp}						`+3P` `+Masc` `+Sg`
T_{voc}		a		a		
T_{vocp}						`+Act`

...

Table 1: *A possible alignment of 8 tapes to capture Arabic verbal morphology.*

can provide this information by virtue of its construction. The above example could in an 8-tape automaton encoding be captured as illustrated in table 1, assuming here that T_{input} is the input tape, the content of which is provided, and the subsequent tapes are output tapes where the parse appears.

In table 1, we see that the radicals on the *root* tape are aligned with the input, as is the pattern on the *pattern* tape, the suffix *-a* on the suffix tape, which again is aligned with the parse for the suffix on the affix parse tape ($affp$), and finally the vocalization *a* is aligned with the input and the pattern. This is very much in tune with both the type of analyses linguists seem to prefer (McCarthy, 1981), and more traditional analyses and lexicography of root-and-pattern languages such as Arabic.

In what follows, we will present an alternate encoding for multi-tape automata together with an implementation of an analyzer for Arabic verbal morphology. The encoding simulates a multi-tape automaton using a simple one-tape finite-state machine and can be implemented using standard toolkits and algorithms given in the literature. The encoding also avoids the abovementioned blow-up problems related to symbol combinations on multiple tapes.

2 Notation

We assume the reader is familiar with the basic notation regarding finite automata and regular expressions. We will use the standard operators of Kleene closure (L^*), union ($L_1 \cup L_2$), intersection ($L_1 \cap L_2$), and assume concatenation whenever there is no overt operator specified ($L_1 L_2$). We use the symbol Σ to specify the alphabet, and the shorthand $\backslash a$ to denote any symbol in the alphabet except a. Slight additional notation will be introduced in the course of elaborating the model.

3 Encoding

In our implementation, we have decided to encode the multi-tape automaton functionality as consisting of a single string read by a single-tape automaton, where the multiple tapes are all evenly interleaved. The first symbol corresponds to the first symbol on tape 1, the second to the first on tape 2, etc.:

T_1	$\downarrow$	$\downarrow$	$\downarrow$

...

T_{n-1}	$\downarrow$	$\downarrow$	$\downarrow$
T_n	$\nearrow$	$\nearrow$	$\downarrow$

...

For instance, the two-tape correspondence:

T_1	a	
T_2	b	c

would be encoded as the string $ab\varepsilon c$, ε being a special symbol used to pad the blanks on a tape to keep all tapes synchronized.

This means that, for example, for an 8-tape representation, every 8th symbol from the beginning is a symbol representing tape 1.

Although this is the final encoding we wish to produce, we have added one extra temporary feature to facilitate the construction: every symbol on any 'tape' is always preceded by a symbol indicating the tape number drawn from an alphabet $T_1, \ldots, T_n$. These symbols are removed eventually. That means that during the construction, the above two-tape example would be represented by the string $T_1 a T_2 b T_1 \varepsilon T_2 c$. This simple redundancy mechanism will ease the writing of grammars and actually limit the size of intermediate automata during construction.

4 Construction

4.1 Overview

We construct a finite-state n-tape simulation grammar in two steps. Firstly we populate each 'tape' with all grammatically possible strings. That means that, for our Arabic example, the root tape should contain all possible roots we wish to accept, the template tape all the possible templates, etc. We call this language the Base. The second step is to constrain the co-occurrence of symbols on the individual tapes, i.e. a consonant on the root tape must be matched by a consonant of the input tape as well as the symbol `C` on the pattern tape, etc. Our grammar then consists of all the permitted combinations of tape symbols allowed by a) the `Base` and b) the `Rules`. The resulting language is simply their intersection, viz.:

$$\text{Base} \cap \text{Rules}$$

4.2 Populating the tapes

We have three auxiliary functions, `TapeL(X,Y)`, `TapeM(X,Y)`, and `TapeA(X,Y)`, where the argument `X` is the tape number, and `Y` the language we with to insert on tape `X`.[3] `TapeL(X,Y)` creates strings where every symbol from the language `Y` is preceded by the tape indicator T_X and where the entire tape is left-aligned, meaning there are no initial blanks on that tape. `TapeM` is the same function, except words on that tape can be preceded by blanks and succeeded by blanks. `TapeA` allows for any alignment of blanks within words or to the left or right. Hence, to illustrate this behavior, `TapeL(4,C V C V C)` will produce strings like:

$$\mathtt{X}T_4\mathbf{C}\mathtt{X}T_4\mathbf{V}\mathtt{X}T_4\mathbf{C}\mathtt{X}T_4\mathbf{V}\mathtt{X}T_4\mathbf{C}\mathtt{Y}$$

where `X` is any sequence of symbols not containing the symbol T_4, and `Y` any sequence possibly containing T_4 but where T_4 is always followed by ε, i.e. we pad all tapes at the end to allow for synchronized strings on other tapes containing more material to the right.

Now, if, as in our grammar, tape 4 is the template tape, we would populate that tape by declaring the language:

```
TapeM(4,Templates)
```

assuming `Templates` is the language that accepts all legal template strings, e.g. `CVCVC`, `CVCCVC`, etc.

Hence, our complete `Base` language (continuing with the 8-tape example) is:

```
TapeL(1,Inputs)         ∩
TapeA(2,Roots)          ∩
TapeL(3,Forms)          ∩
TapeM(4,Templates)      ∩
TapeA(5,Affixes)        ∩
TapeM(6,Parses)         ∩
TapeA(7,Voc)            ∩
TapeL(8,VocParses)      ∩
```

$$(T_1\Sigma T_2\Sigma T_3\Sigma T_4\Sigma T_5\Sigma T_6\Sigma T_7\Sigma T_8\Sigma)^*$$

This will produce the language where all strings are multiples of 16 in length. Every other symbol is the T_X tape marker symbol and every other symbol is the actual symbol on that tape (allowing for the special symbol ε also to represent blanks on a tape). Naturally, we will want to define `Inputs` occurring on tape 1 as any string containing any combination of symbols since it represents all possible input words we wish to parse. Similarly, tape 2 will contain all possible roots, etc. This `Base` language is subsequently constrained so that symbols on different tapes align correctly and are only allowed if they represent a legal parse of the word on the input tape (tape 1).

4.3 Constructing the rules

When constructing the rules that constrain the co-occurrence of symbols on the various tapes we shall primarily take advantage of the $\Rightarrow$ operator first introduced for two-level grammars by Koskenniemi (1983).[4] The semantics is as follows. A statement:

$$X \Rightarrow L_1 \;\_\; R_1, \ldots, L_n \;\_\; R_n$$

where X and L_i, R_i are all regular languages defines the regular language where every instance of a substring drawn from the language X must be surrounded by some pair L_i and R_i to the left and right, respectively.[5]

Indeed, all of our rules will consist exclusively of $\Rightarrow$ statements.

To take an example: in order to constrain the template we need two rules that effectively say that every C and V symbol occurring in the template

[3]See the appendix for exact definitions of these functions.

[4]There is a slight, but subtle difference in notation, though: the original two-level $\Rightarrow$ operator constrained single symbols only (such as $a{:}b$, which was considered at compile-time a single symbol); here, the argument X refers to any arbitrary language.

[5]Many finite-state toolkits contain this as a separate operator. See Yli-Jyrä and Koskenniemi (2004) and Hulden (2008) for how such statements can be converted into regular expressions and finite automata.

tape must be matched by 1) a consonant on the root tape and 2) a vowel on the input tape. Because of our single-tape encoding the first rule translates to the idea that every T_4 C sequence must be directly preceded by T_2 followed by some consonant followed by T_3 and any symbol at all:

$$T_4\ C\ \Rightarrow\ T_2\ \texttt{Cons}\ T_3\ \Sigma\ \_ \qquad (1)$$

and the second one translates to:

$$T_4\ V\ \Rightarrow\ T_1\ \texttt{Vow}\ T_2\ \Sigma\ T_3\ \Sigma\ \_ \qquad (2)$$

assuming that `Vow` is the language that contains any vowel and `Cons` the language that contains any consonant.

Similarly, we want to constrain the `Forms` parse tape that contains symbols such as `Form_I`, `Form_II` etc., so that if, for example, `Form_I` occurs on that tape, the pattern `CVCVC` must occur on the pattern tape.[6]

$$T_3\,\texttt{Form\_I} \Rightarrow \_\,\texttt{TapeM(4,C V C V C)} \qquad (3)$$

and likewise for all the other forms. It should be noted that most constraints are very strictly local to within a few symbols, depending slightly on the ordering and function of the tapes. In (1), for instance, which constrains a symbol on tape 4 with a consonant on tape 2, there are only 2 intervening symbols, namely that of tape 3. The ordering of the tapes thus has some bearing on both how simple the rules are to write, and the size of the resulting automaton. Naturally, tapes that constrain each other are ideally placed in adjacent positions whenever possible.

Of course, some long-distance constraints will be inevitable. For example, Form II is generally described as a `CVCCVC` pattern, where the extra consonant is a geminate, as in the stem `kattab`, where the *t* of the root associates with both `C`'s in the pattern. To distinguish this `C` behavior from that of Form X which is also commonly described with two adjacent `C` symbols where, however, there is no such association (as in the stem *staktab*) we need to introduce another symbol. This symbol $\texttt{C}_2$ occurs in Form II, which becomes $\texttt{CVCC}_2\texttt{VC}$. We then introduce a constraint to the effect that any $\texttt{C}_2$-symbol must be matched on the input by a consonant, which is identical to the previous consonant on the input tape.[7] These long-distance dependencies can be avoided to some extent by grammar engineering, but so long as they do not cause a combinatorial explosion in the number of states of the resulting grammar automaton, we have decided to include them for the sake of clarity.

To give an overview of some of the subsequent constraints that are still necessary, we include here a few descriptions and examples (where the starred (***) tape snippets exemplify illegal configurations):

- Every root consonant has a matching consonant on the input tape

T_1	k	a	t	a	b	a
T_2	k		t		b	
T_1	k	a	t	a	b	a
T_2***	d		r		s	

- A vowel in the input which is matched by a V in the pattern, must have a corresponding vocalization vowel

T_1	k	a	t	a	b	a
T_4	C	V	C	V	C	
T_7		a		a		
T_1	k	a	t	a	b	a
T_4	C	V	C	V	C	
T_7***		u		i		

- A position where there is a symbol in the input either has a symbol in the pattern tape or a symbol in the affix tape (but not both)

T_1	k	a	t	a	b	a
T_4	C	V	C	V	C	
T_5						a
T_1	k	a	t	a	b	a
T_4	C	V	C	V	C	
T_5***						

[6] To be more exact, to be able to match and parse both fully vocalized words such as *wadarasat* (وَدَرَسَتْ), and unvocalized ones, such as *wdrst* (ودرست), we want the pattern `CVCVC` to actually be represented by the regular expression `C (V) C (V) C`, i.e. where the vowels are optional. Note, however, that the rule that constrains T_4 V above only requires that the V matches *if* there indeed is one. Hence, by declaring vowels in patterns (and vocalizations) to be optional, we can always parse any partially, fully, or unvocalized verb. Of course, fully unvocalized words will be much more ambiguous and yield more parses.

[7] The idea to preserve the gemination in the grammar is similar to the solutions regarding gemination and spreading of Forms II, V, and IX documented in Beesley (1998b) and Habash and Rambow (2006).

4.4 The final automaton

As mentioned above, the symbols $\{T_1, \ldots, T_n\}$ are only used during construction of the automaton for the convenience of writing the grammar, and shall be removed after intersecting the Base language with the Rules languages. This is a simple substitution $T_X \rightarrow \epsilon$, i.e. the empty string. Hence, the grammar is compiled as:

$$\texttt{Grammar} = h(\texttt{Base} \cap \texttt{Rules})$$

where h is a homomorphism that replaces T_X symbols with ϵ, the empty string.

5 Efficiency Considerations

Because the construction method proposed can very quickly produce automata of considerable size, there are a few issues to consider when designing a grammar this way. Of primary concern is that since one is constructing deterministic automata, long-distance constraints should be kept to a minimum. Local constraints, which the majority of grammar rules encode, yield so-called k-testable languages when represented as finite automata, and the state complexity of their intersection grows additively. For larger k, however, growth is more rapid which means that, for example, when one is designing the content of the individual tapes, care should be taken to ensure that segments or symbols which are related to each other preferably align very closely on the tapes. Naturally, this same goal is of linguistic interest as well and a grammar which does not align grammatical information with segments in the input is likely not a good grammar. However, there are a couple of ways in which one can go astray. For instance, in the running example we have presented, one of the parse tapes has included the symbol `+3P +Masc +Sg`, aligned with the affix that represents the grammatical information:

...

T_5						a

T_6						`+3P`
						`+Masc`
						`+Sg`

...

However, if it be the case that what the parse tape reflects is a prefix or a circumfix, as will be the case with the imperfective, subjunctive and jussive forms, the following alignment would be somewhat inefficient:

...

T_5	t	a						

T_6								`+3P`
								`+Fem`
								`+Sg`

...

This is because the prefix *ta*, which appears early in the word, is reflected on tape 6 at the end of the word, in effect unnecessarily producing a very long-distance dependency and hence duplicates of states in the automaton encoding the intervening material. A more efficient strategy is to place the parse or annotation tape material as close as possible to the segments which have a bearing on it, i.e.:

...

T_5	t	a						

T_6	`+3P`
	`+Fem`
	`+Sg`							

...

This alignment can be achieved by a constraint in the grammar to the effect that the first non-blank symbol on the affix tape is in the same position as the first non-blank symbol on the affix parse tape.

It is also worth noting that our implementation does not yet restrict the co-occurrence of roots and forms, i.e. it will parse any word in any root in the lexicon in any of the forms I-VIII, X. Adding these restrictions will presumably produce some growth in the automaton. However, for the time being we have also experimented with accepting any triliteral root—i.e. any valid consonantal combination. This has drastically cut the size of the resulting automaton to only roughly 2,000 states without much overgeneration in the sense that words will not incorrectly be matched with the wrong root. The reason for this small footprint when not having a 'real' lexicon is fairly obvious—all dependencies between the root tape and the pattern tape and the input tape are instantly resolved in the span of one 'column' or 7 symbols.

6 Algorithmic additions

Naturally, one can parse words by simply intersecting `TapeL(1, word)` $\cap$ `Grammar`, where `word` is the word at hand and printing out all the legal strings. Still, this is unwieldy because of the intersection operation involved and for faster lookup speeds one needs to consider an algorithmic extension that performs this lookup directly on the `Grammar` automaton.

6.1 Single-tape transduction

For our implementation, we have simply modified the automaton matching algorithm in the toolkit we have used, *foma*[8] to, instead of matching every symbol, matching the first symbol as the 'input', then outputting the subsequent n (where n is 7 in our example) legal symbols if the subsequent input symbols match. Because the grammar is quite constrained, this produces very little temporary ambiguity in the depth-first search traversal of the automaton and transduces an input to the output tapes in nearly linear time.

7 Future work

The transduction mechanism mentioned above works well and is particularly easy to implement when the first 'tape' is the input tape containing the word one wants to parse, since one can simply do a depth-first search until the the next symbol on the input tape (in our running example with 8 tapes, that would be 7 symbols forward) and discard the paths where the subsequent tape 1 symbols do not match, resulting in nearly linear running time. However, for the generation problem, the solution is less obvious. If one wanted to supply any of the other tapes with a ready input (such as form, root, and a combination of grammatical categories), and then yield a string on tape 1, the problem would be more difficult. Naturally, one can intersect various TapeX(n, content) languages against the grammar, producing all the possible input strings that could have generated such a parse, but this method is rather slow and results only in a few parses per second on our system. Devising a fast algorithm to achieve this would be desirable for applications where one wanted to, for instance, generate all possible vocalization patterns in a given word, or for IR purposes where one would automatically apply vocalizations to Arabic words.

[8] See the appendix.

8 Conclusion

We have described a straightforward method by which morphological analyzers for languages that exhibit root-and-pattern morphology can be built using standard finite-state methods to simulate multi-tape automata. This enables one to take advantage of already widely available standard toolkits designed for construction of single-tape automata or finite-state transducers. The feasibility of the approach has been tested with a limited implementation of Arabic verbal morphology that contains roughly 2,000 roots, yielding automata of manageable size. With some care in construction the method should be readily applicable to larger projects in Arabic and other languages, in particular to languages that exhibit root-and-pattern or templatic morphologies.

References

Beesley, K. and Karttunen, L. (2003). *Finite-State Morphology*. CSLI, Stanford.

Beesley, K. R. (1996). Arabic finite-state analysis and generation. In *COLING '96*.

Beesley, K. R. (1998a). Arabic morphology using only finite-state operations. In *Proceedings of the Workshop on Computational Approaches to Semitic Languages COLING-ACL*, pages 50–57.

Beesley, K. R. (1998b). Consonant spreading in Arabic stems. In *ACL*, volume 36, pages 117–123. Association for Computational Linguistics.

Beeston, A. F. L. (1968). *Written Arabic: An approach to the basic structures*. Cambridge University Press, Cambridge.

Buckwalter, T. (2004). Arabic morphological analyzer 2.0. *LDC*.

Habash, N. and Rambow, O. (2006). MAGEAD: A morphological analyzer and generator for the Arabic dialects. *Proceedings of COLING-ACL 2006*.

Habash, N., Rambow, O., and Kiraz, G. (2005). Morphological analysis and generation for Arabic dialects. *Proceedings of the Workshop on Computational Approaches to Semitic Languages (ACL '05)*.

Hulden, M. (2008). Regular expressions and predicate logic in finite-state language processing.

In Piskorski, J., Watson, B., and Yli-Jyrä, A., editors, *Proceedings of FSMNLP 2008*.

Kataja, L. and Koskenniemi, K. (1988). Finite-state description of Semitic morphology: a case study of ancient Akkadian. In *COLING '88*, pages 313–315.

Kay, M. (1987). Nonconcatenative finite-state morphology. In *Proceedings of the third conference on European chapter of the Association for Computational Linguistics*, pages 2–10. Association for Computational Linguistics.

Kiraz, G. A. (1994). Multi-tape two-level morphology: A case study in Semitic non-linear morphology. In *COLING '94*, pages 180–186.

Kiraz, G. A. (2000). Multi-tiered nonlinear morphology using multitape finite automata: A case study on Syriac and Arabic. *Computational Linguistics*, 26(1):77–105.

Kiraz, G. A. (2001). *Computational nonlinear morphology: with emphasis on Semitic languages*. Cambridge University Press, Cambridge.

Koskenniemi, K. (1983). *Two-level morphology: A general computational model for word-form recognition and production*. Publication 11, University of Helsinki, Department of General Linguistics, Helsinki.

Lavie, A., Itai, A., and Ornan, U. (1988). On the applicability of two level morphology to the inflection of Hebrew verbs. In *Proceedings of ALLC III*, pages 246–260.

McCarthy, J. J. (1981). A Prosodic Theory of Nonconcatenative Morphology. *Linguistic Inquiry*, 12(3):373–418.

van Noord, G. (2000). *FSA 6 Reference Manual*.

Wehr, H. (1979). *A Dictionary of Modern Written Arabic*. Spoken Language Services, Inc., Ithaca, NY.

Yli-Jyrä, A. and Koskenniemi, K. (2004). Compiling contextual restrictions on strings into finite-state automata. *The Eindhoven FASTAR Days Proceedings*.

Yona, S. and Wintner, S. (2008). A finite-state morphological grammar of Hebrew. *Natural Language Engineering*, 14(2):173–190.

9 Appendix

The practical implementation described in the paper was done with the freely available (GNU Licence) *foma* finite-state toolkit.[9]. However, all of the techniques used are available in other toolkits as well, such as *xfst* (Beesley and Karttunen, 2003), or *fsa* (van Noord, 2000)), and translation of the notation should be straightforward.

The functions for populating the tapes in section 4.2, were defined in *foma* as follows:

```
TapeL(X,Y) =
[[Y ∘ [[0×\X \X]* [0×X] ∑]*]2
[X ε|\X \X]*]
TapeM(X,Y) = [[Y ∘ [0×[\X \X|X ε]]*
[0×\X \X]* [0×X] ∑]*]2 [X ε|\X \X]*]
TapeA(X,Y) = [[Y ∘
[0×\X \X|X ε]* 0×X ∑]*]2;
```

Here, TapeX is a function of two variables, X and Y. Transducer composition is denoted by $\circ$, cross-product by $\times$, the lower projection of a relation by L_2, and union by $|$. Brackets indicate grouping and Σ any symbol. The notation $\backslash X$ denotes any single symbol, except X. The symbol ε here is the special 'blank' symbol used to pad the tapes and keep them synchronized.

[9] http://foma.sourceforge.net

A Hybrid Approach for Building Arabic Diacritizer

Khaled Shaalan
The Faculty of Informatics
The British University in Dubai
khaled.shaalan@buid.ac.ae

Hitham M. Abo Bakr
Computer & System Dept
Zagazig University
hithamab@yahoo.com

Ibrahim Ziedan
Computer & System Dept.
Zagazig University
i.ziedan@yahoo.com

Abstract

Modern standard Arabic is usually written without diacritics. This makes it difficult for performing Arabic text processing. Diacritization helps clarify the meaning of words and disambiguate any vague spellings or pronunciations, as some Arabic words are spelled the same but differ in meaning. In this paper, we address the issue of adding diacritics to undiacritized Arabic text using a hybrid approach. The approach requires an Arabic lexicon and large corpus of fully diacritized text for training purposes in order to detect diacritics. Case-Ending is treated as a separate post processing task using syntactic information. The hybrid approach relies on lexicon retrieval, bigram, and SVM-statistical prioritized techniques. We present results of an evaluation of the proposed diacritization approach and discuss various modifications for improving the performance of this approach.

1 Introduction

Modern Arabic written texts usually include Arabic scripts without short vowels and other diacritic marks. This often leads to considerable ambiguity since several words that have different diacritic patterns may appear identical in a diacritic-less setting. Educated modern Arabic speakers are able to accurately derive/restore diacritics in a document. This is based on the context and their linguistic knowledge of Arabic. However, a text without diacritics brings difficulties for Arabic readers. It is also problematic for Arabic processing applications, such as text-to-speech, speech-to-text, and text analysis, where the lack of diacritics adds another layer of ambiguity when processing the input data. As an example, full vocalization of Arabic text is required for text-to-speech applications, where the mapping from graphemes to phonemes is complicated compared to languages such as English and French; where there is, in most cases, simple one-to-one relationship. Nevertheless, using Arabic text with diacritics has proven an improvement in the accuracy of speech-recognition applications (Zitouni et al., 2006).

The problem of automatic restoration (i.e., derivation) of the diacritic signs of Arabic text can be solved by two approaches. The first is a rule-based approach that involves a complex integration of the Arabic morphological, syntactic, and semantic tools with significant efforts to acquire respective linguistic rules. A morphological analyzer gets the breakdowns of the undiacritized word according to known patterns or templates and recognizes its prefixes and suffixes. A syntax analyzer applies specific syntactic rules to determine the case-ending diacritics, usually, by techniques such as finite-state automata. Semantics handling helps to resolve ambiguous cases and to filter out hypothesis. Hence, rule-based diacritization approach is a complicated process and takes longer time to process an Arabic sentence which is naturally long. The second approach is the statistical approach that requires linguistic resources such as a large tagged corpus (in particular a TreeBank) to extract language statistics for estimating the missing diacritical marks. The approach is fully automated and does not require efforts to acquire respective linguistic knowledge. Results are usually improved by increasing the size of the corpus.

It is worth noting that identifying some of the diacritic marks can be seen as a morphological problem and the relevant letters are called internal characters in this paper. Moreover, diacritic mark of the last character of the Arabic is called case ending (علامة الاعراب). The identification of case-ending diacritics is determined at the syn-

Proceedings of the EACL 2009 Workshop on Computational Approaches to Semitic Languages, pages 27–35,
Athens, Greece, 31 March, 2009. ©2009 Association for Computational Linguistics

tactic processing level (case ending depends on the position of the word within the sentence) whereas detecting the internal diacritics is determined at the morphological processing level. In widespread cases, the case-ending come internally rather than with the last character such as "بقلمها" (by-her-pen).

In this paper, an Arabic diacritizer is proposed. Internal diacritization was restored by a model based on the synergy of three different techniques: retrieval of unambiguous lexicon entries, retrieval of two-word expression from a preprocessed diacritized bigram database, and a prediction using statistical approach based on SVM-learning technique, (Cristianini and Taylor, 2000) and (Hearst, 1998). The later technique tokenizes a text and provides a Reduced Tag Set (RTS) of Part of Speech (POS)[1] for each token. The tags are used to restore the diacritics. From the obtained diacritization results of these techniques, the most consistent one is selected.

The Case-Ending diacritization is treated as a post-process of the internal diacritization task using the same machine learning approach that was trained on Base phrase (BP)-Chunk as well as POS features of individual tokens with correct case-ending tags. A utility has been designed to extract correct case-ending tags from the LDC's Arabic Tree Bank (ATB).

This paper presents a new simple but efficient approach that gets results comparable with the best performing systems, to our knowledge, (Habash and Rambow, 2007). The achieved results are: 11.795% Word Error Rate (WER) and about 3.245% Diacritics Error Rate (DER). The paper is structured as follows. Section 2 reviews closely related work. Section 3 introduces the proposed diacritization approach. Section 4 describes the training process. Section 5 presents the evaluation experiment. Section 6 concludes the article and gives direction for future research.

2 Related Work

Diacritic restoration has been receiving increasing attention and has been the focus of several studies. In El-Sadany and Hashish (1988), a rule-based approach that uses morphological analyzer for vowelization was proposed. Another, rule-based grapheme to sound conversion approach appeared in 2003 by Y. El-Imam (2003).
There are many related works dealing with the problem of Arabic diacritization in general (Zitouni et al., 2006), (Habash and Rambow, 2007), (Ananthakrishnan, 2005), (Kirchhoff, 2005). and (Elshafei et al, 2006); all trying to handle this problem using statistical approaches but they tend to handle the case ending diacritic mark in the same way they used to handle the internal (any letter but the last) diacritics. In our proposed approach we differentiate between them as the detection of case-ending diacritics is a syntactic-based problem whereas detecting the internal diacritics is a morphological-based problem. Habash et al. (2007) introduced a system called MADA-D that uses Buckwalter's Arabic morphological analyzer where they used 14 taggers and a lexeme-based language model. MADA is so far the best performing system to date. It has been reported that it achieved a WER of 14.9% and a DER of 4.8%.

3 The Proposed Diacritization Approach

The Arabic internal diacritization problem will be addressed from three different proposed techniques, each of which has its own strengths and weaknesses. Such techniques are integrated to optimize the performance of the Arabic diacritizer and to a large extent remove ambiguities. These proposed techniques are: 1) Lexicon Retrieval, 2) diacritized bigram, and 3) SVM-statistical-based diacritizer. Then, the case ending diacritization will be determined after the internal discrimination is performed. Figure 1 shows the architecture of Arabic Diacritization System.

[1] List of POS and RTS that are used here can be found at: http://www.ircs.upenn.edu/arabic/Jan03release/arabic-POStags-collapse-to-PennPOStags.txt

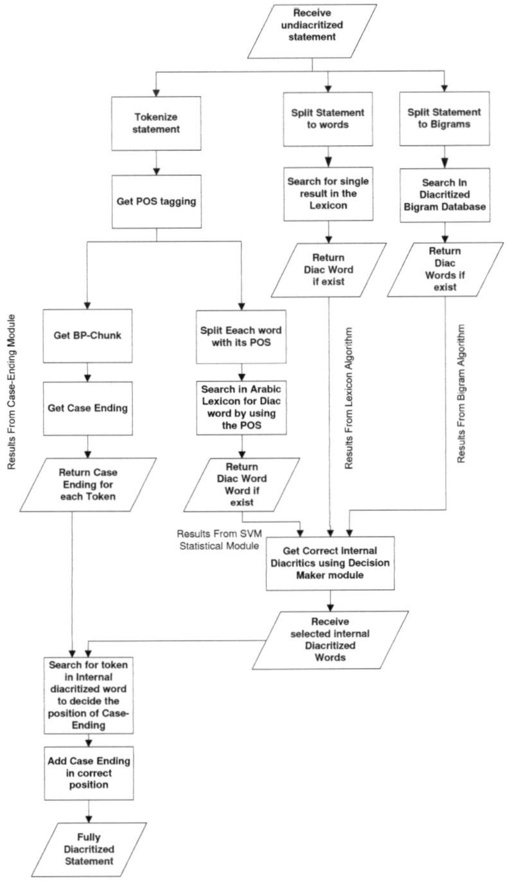

Figure 1: Arabic Diacritization System

Lexicon Retrieval Technique (LR)

Lexicon retrieval approach tries to find the result (diacritized word) returned from an Arabic lexicon for a specific input undiacritized word. If only one diacritization is returned, then there is no ambiguity. This solution is final and we do not need to look at the results form the other two techniques. However, this situation is usually rare but when it occurs the result is confirmed.

Diacritized Bigram Technique (DB)

When more than one solution is retrieved for an unvowelized input word, i.e., ambiguous diacrticazation, the bigram technique comes into play. The idea behind this technique is to make use of the multiword expressions in Arabic texts. When such expressions are analyzed as separate words, the possibility for ambiguity is increased. In this work, we considered a two-word expression (bigram) that usually occurs with high frequency in Arabic texts such that one word can determine the diacritization of the other. Once the expression is identified and diacritized correctly, it adds a sense of certitude to the diacritization which significantly reduces the ambiguity. Table 1 shows an extraction of the diacritized bigram database.

Diac. 2nd Word	Diac. 1st Word	Cat	2nd Word	1st Word
القَدَم	لِكُرَة	3	القدم	لكرة
المُتَّحِدَة	الولايات	1	المتحدة	الولايات
الوُزَراء	رَئِيس	1	الوزراء	رئيس
برس	فرانْس	1	برس	فرانس
الغَرْبِيَّة	الضِفّة	1	الغربية	الضفة

Table 1: Diacritized Bigram Database

SVM-Statistical Technique (SVM)

The previous two diacritization techniques can be viewed as a lookup process; either for a word in the lexicon or for a two-word expression in a large bigram database. However, statistical methods can be viewed as general approaches because they are heavily dependent on the Arabic syntactic analysis that was manually performed by Arabic specialists.

The main idea of this approach is to tokenize and automatically annotate tokens with the correct POS tags. Then, by searching the Arabic lexicon using a token and the corresponding POS, the correct diacritization result can reached, even though multiple ambiguous words are retrieved from the lexicon.

Buckwalter's morphological analyzer (Buckwalter, 2002) takes an inflected Arabic word and returns fully diacritized ambiguous words. We claim in our approach that only internal diacritics should be handled morphologically whereas case ending should be handled syntactically. Hence, we have used the Buckwalter's morphological analyzer after removing all case ending diacritics from the suffixes table in order to prevent the generation of the case ending output. One advantage of this modification is to considerably reduce the number of alternatives (i.e., overgenerations) returned from the morphological analyzer. Another advantage is that some NLP tasks, such as Information Retrieval, require only diacritic restoration of internal (lexical) vowels which can benefit from such modification. For example, given the word " عامل " to this morphological analyzer, it returns 7 results that have the same internal diacritics with one having no case-ending and 6 having different case-ending diacritics. Consequently, splitting the diacrization into two stages (internal and case ending) will avoid such morphological ambiguity and at the second stage the syntactic case ending is treated separately as a post processing which ultimately leads to a fully efficient diacritized Arabic word.

A Hybrid of All Internal Techniques

When we apply each of the three proposed techniques on an input undiacritized Arabic sentence we may get different diacritization results for each word within this sentence. The selection criteria depend on the agreement among these techniques. Two or more matched results can determine the discrimination of a word. In case of disagreement, a priority is applied in the following, highest to lowest, order: lexicon retrieval, bigram and SVM-Statistical technique respectively. If no solution is reached from all techniques, the undiacritized input word is returned.

Case Ending Model

The main idea is to relate the case-ending for each token with its POS and chunk position as well as its position within the sentence (Abo Bakr et al., 2008). We made a training using Support Vector Machines (SVM) technique with undiacritized tokens. This technique involves an Arabic Treebank.

An Arabic Treebank usually created on top of a corpus that has already been annotated with POS tags. We have used the Penn Arabic Treebank (ATB) (Maamouri et al, 2004). ATB has begun in the fall of 2001 and has now completed four full releases of morphologically and syntactically annotated data: Version 1 of the ATB has three parts with different releases; some versions like Part 1 V3.0 and Part 2 V 2.0 are fully diacritized trees. For example, consider the following undiacritized statement:

"لليوم الثاني على التوالي تظاهر طلاب ينتمون الى جماعة...."

"llvwm AlvAnv ElY AltwAlv tZAhr TlAb

The following tree representation is partially extracted from the tree fileU-MAAH_UM.ARB_20020120-a.0007.tree that is part of the ATB Part 2 V.2.

```
(S (S (S (PP-TMP (PREP li-) (NP (NP
(DET+NOUN+CASE_DEF_GEN -Al+yawom+i)
(DET+ADJ Al+vAniy)) (PP (PREP EalaY) (NP
(DET+NOUN Al+tawAliy))))) (VP
(VERB_PERFECT+PVSUFF_SUBJ:3MS N
Al+musolim+iyona) .....
```

Figure 2 shows a graphical representation of this tree[2]. Case-ending is indicated, ovals in Figure 2, by one of the following tags: NCE, CASE_DEF_GEN, CASE_INDEF_GEN, CASE_DEF_NOM, CASE_DEF_ACC, CASE_INDEF_NOM, CASE_DEF_ACCGEN, CASE_INDEF ACC, and CASE_INDEF_ACCGEN.

Table 2 gives the complete description of these tags.

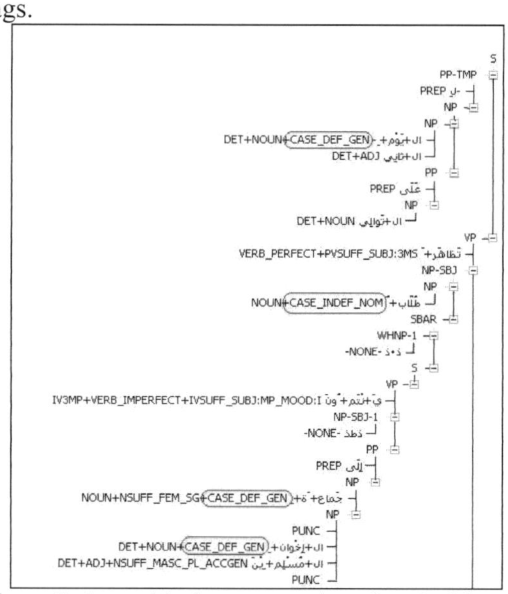

Figure 2: A graphical representation of an Arabic sentence extracted from the Penn Arabic Treebank

Case Ending Tags	**Description**
NCE	No Case Ending
CASE_DEF_GEN	Kasra ِ
CASE_INDEF_GEN	kasratan ٍ
CASE_DEF_NOM	Damma ُ
CASE_DEF_ACC	Fat-ha َ
CASE_DEF_ACCGEN	Maftouh bi Kasra ِ
CASE_INDEF_NOM	Damatan ٌ
CASE_INDEF_ACCGEN	Fathatan ً or ٍ
CASE_INDEF_ACC	Fathatan ً

Table 2: Description of Case-Ending tags found in ATB

A sequence of tokens with its POS, BP-chunk and Case-Ending is extracted from Treebank using YamCha File Creator (YFC utility[3]). The

[2] This graphical representation of the Treebank files is extracted from our Treebank Viewer tool that is freely available at: http://www.staff.zu.edu.eg/hmabobakr/

[3] We developed YFC utility to extract information from Penn Arabic Treebank ATB and produce the Yamcha standard input format to be able to use this information in the training process. http://www.staff.zu.edu.eg/hmabobakr/page.asp?id=53

basic approach used in YFC is inspired by the work of Sabine for Treebank-to-chuck conversion script (Sang and Buchholz, 2000), which we have extended to be used with Arabic. This has required adding some features like Case-Ending. The output produced from YFC utility for case ending training process is shown in Table 3.

Token	POS	Chunk	Case Ending
L	IN	B-PP	NCE
Al	DT	B-NP	NCE
ywm	NN	I-NP	CASE_DEF_GEN
Al	DT	I-NP	NCE
vAny	JJ	I-NP	NCE
ElY	IN	B-PP	NCE
Al	DT	B-NP	NCE
twAly	NN	I-NP	NCE
tZAhr	VBD	B-VP	NCE
TlAb	NN	B-NP	CASE_INDEF_NOM
Yntmwn	VBP	B-VP	NCE
<lY	IN	B-PP	NCE
jmAEp	NN	B-NP	CASE_DEF_GEN

Table 3: Training file format for detecting Case-Ending

4 Training of the Arabic Diacritizer

The diacritization system we present here is trained and evaluated on the LDC's Arabic Treebank of diacritized news articles – Part 2 v2.0: catalog number LDC2004T02 and 1-58563-282-1. The corpus includes complete vocalization (including case endings). We introduce here a clearly defined and replicable split of the corpus, so that the reproduction of the results or future investigations can accurately and correctly be established. This corpus includes 501 stories from the Ummah Arabic News Text. There are a total of 144,199 words (counting non-Arabic tokens such as numbers and punctuation) in the 501 files - one story per file. We split the corpus into two sets: training data and development test (devtest) data. The devtest data are the files ended by character "7" like "UMAAH_UM.ARB_20020120-a.0007.tree" and its count was 38 files. The remaining files are used for training.

5 Evaluation

For Arabic tokenizer, POS tagger, BP-chunk, and statistical Case-Ending, we used a standard SVM with a polynomial kernel of degree 2 and C=1.0. Evaluation of the system was done by calculating the performance using the standard evaluation measures: accuracy, precision, recall, and the f-measure[4].We used YamCha (Kudo and Matsumoto, 2003) implementation of SVMs. Diacritization evaluation of our experiments is reported in terms of word error rate (WER), and diacritization error rate (DER)[5].

We conducted experiments to:

1. Evaluate the impact of tokenization, part-of-speech, chunking, and case-ending parameters on the training models, see Section 5.1.
2. Evaluate the impact of including and excluding the case-ending on the performance of the Arabic diacritizer, see Section 5.2.
3. Compare our approach of Tokenization and POS tagger with the ArabicSVMTools tagger using different parameters and feature(s), see Section 5.2.

5.1 Results of Tokenization, Part-of-Speech, BP-chunking, and case-ending

The results obtained for tokenization (TOK), part-of-speech (POS), and Chunking (BP-chunk) tasks are comparable with the results presented in the most notable literature (Diab et al, 2007; Diab et al, 2004). We did some modifications of the feature list to compromise between the speed and accuracy. The case ending task is novel, and did not get enough handling in other research. It achieved acceptable results.

Evaluation of the impact of the tokenization parameter on the training process

Two tokenization tasks was performed on window sizes of -2 /+2 and -4/+4, for illustration see TOK1 and TOK2 tasks in Figure 3. For each window size there are two columns. The first one contains a sequence of Buckwalter's transliterated Arabic letters shown from top to bottom that resembles the left-to-right Arabic writing system (e.g., ...wyblg Eddhm ..... are the transliteration of the Arabic words ...وبيلغ عددهم..., respectively). The second column contains the corresponding tokenization tags presented by **I**nside-**O**utside-**B**eginning (I-O-B) of a chunk, i.e.,

[4] These results were computed using our developed evluation tool that was developed and tested against Evaluation Tools for CONLL 2000 http://www.cnts.ua.ac.be/conll2000/chunking/conlleval.txt.

[5] These results were computed using our developed evaluation tool that was developed based on information presented in (Habash and Rambow, 2007).

prefix (PRE), word (WRD), and suffix (SUFF), respectively, (Kudo and Matsumoto, 2003). The tokenization tags are: B-PRE1, I-PRE1, B-PRE2, I-PRE2, B-PRE3, I-PRE3, B-WORD-1, I-WORD-1, B-SUFF1, I-SUFF1 and O for outside word boundary. We made segmentation for the determiner "Al" – "ال". This segmentation is important for the case-ending detection for: the adjective and the noun it modifies "الصفة والموصوف", 1st and 2nd Particle of the construction Annexed and Annexed noun "المضاف و المضاف إليه", and Nunation "التنوين". The result of the evaluation of the two tokenization tasks is shown in Table 4.

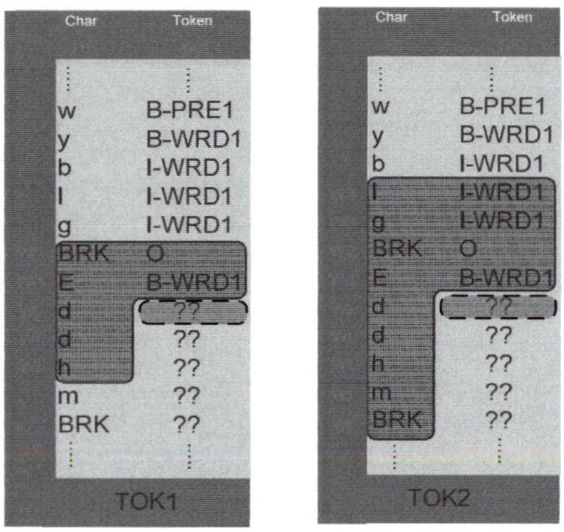

Figure 3: Tokenization evaluation with window sizes of -2/+2 and -4/+4

Measurement	TOK1	TOK2
Accuracy	98.59%	99.56%
Precision	97.17%	98.95%
Recall	97.29%	99.06%
F-Measure	97.23%	99.00%

Table 4: Tokenization results with window sizes of -2/+2 and -4/+4

Evaluation of the impact of the part-of-speech parameter on the training process

A POS tagging (POS1) task was performed on a sequence of tokens produced from the tokenization task. A window size of +2/-2 tokens centered at the focus token. We made another POS tagging (POS2) task by adding the last two characters as an extra feature for enhancing the accuracy of some tags such as plural or dual noun (NNS) and singular noun (NN). For illustration see POS1 and POS2 tasks in Figure 4. The result of the evaluation of the two POS tagging tasks is shown in Table 5.

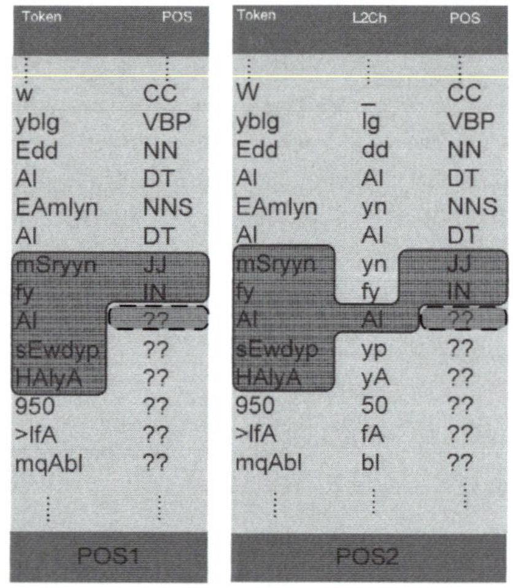

Figure 4: POS evaluations with window size of -2/+2; with and without using the last two characters as an added feature

Measurement	POS1	POS2
Accuracy	94.34%	95.97%

Table 5: POS results for different window sizes

Evaluation of the impact of chunking parameters on the training process

The chunking task was performed on tokens produced from the tokenization and POS tasks. The evaluation included 16 tag-set (features) of a window size of -2/+2 for both tokens and POS, and only the previous two chunk tags. For illustration see Figure 5. The result of the evaluation of is shown in Table 6.

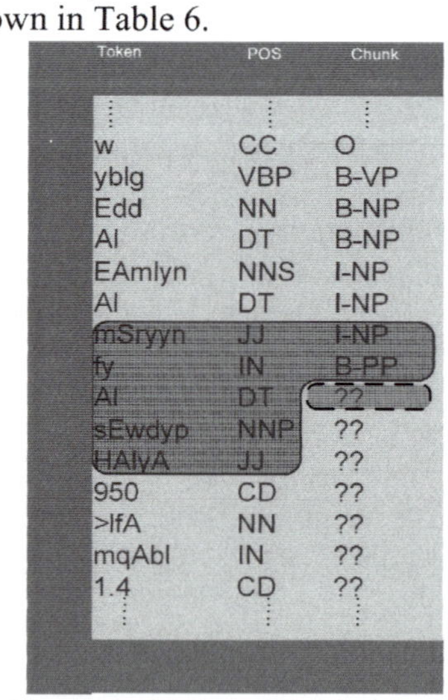

Figure 5: Chunk evaluation with window size of -2/+2

Measurement	Results
Accuracy	95.52%
Precision	93.19%
Recall	95.90%
F-Measure	94.52%

Table 6: Results for BP-chunk

Evaluation of the impact case-ending parameters on the training process

Two case-ending tasks were performed. The first case-ending (CE1) task was discussed in a previous work (Abo Bakr et al., 2008). It was performed on window size of -3/+3 and 8 tag sets. For illustration see Figure 6.

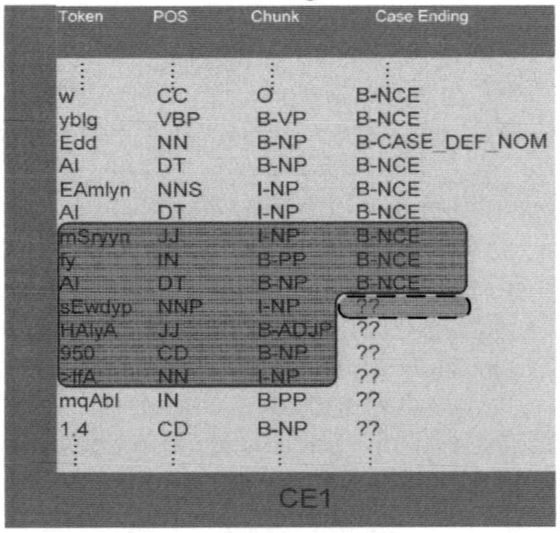

Figure 6: Case-ending evaluation with window size of -3/+3

The evaluation has achieved 95.35% in accuracy. We noticed that in some cases the system can produce unacceptable case ending (e.g., Tanween on the sound plural masculine "جمع المذكر السالم") that we could improved by:

1- Enhancing the POS tagging (POS2) task by adding last two characters (L2Ch) as a feature.
2- Enhancing the case ending (CE2) task by adding the last character (LCh) and the last two characters (L2Ch) as features.

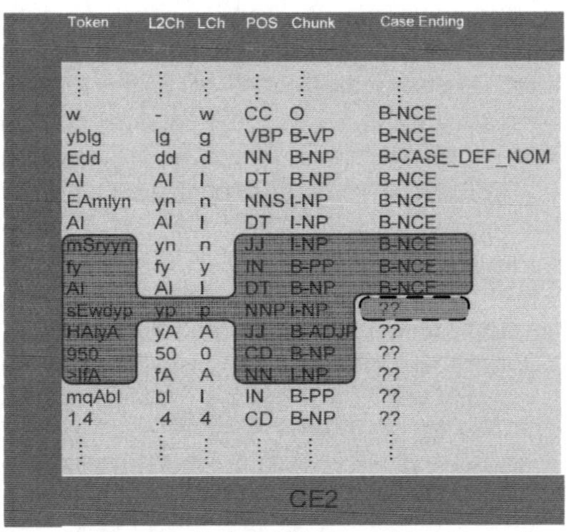

Figure 7: Case-Ending evaluation with widow size of -3/3 and using the last two characters (L2Ch) and the last character (LCh) as added features

The following modifications were done to conduct the second case-ending (CE2) task, for illustration see Figure 7:

- Adding the last two characters (L2Ch) and the last character (LCh) as features.
- Enhancing the case ending representation by adding an extra tagset for "indeclension of the fatha" - "مبني على الفتح" that is presented in Treebank as "PVSUFF_SUNJ:3MS".

Table 7 presents the results obtained for the two case ending (CE1 and CE2) tasks. As shown, the performance is improved.

Measurement	CE1	CE2
Accuracy	95.35%	96.57%

Table 7: Results of Case Ending evaluation

5.2 Diacritization Results

In this section, we compare our approach of Tokenization and POS tagger with ArabicSVMTools tagger. We evaluate the impact of including and excluding different techniques of internal diacritization and case-ending on the overall performance of our Arabic diacritizer. In particular, we show the results from the following techniques: lexicon retrieval (LR), diacritized bigram (DB), SVM, and case-ending (CE), techniques. Results for different combinations were reported and compared. All results were performed using TOK1, POS1, and CE1 tasks and shown in Table 8 through Table 10.

	Including CE		Excluding CE[6]	
Technique	WER	DER	WER	DER
LR	90.35%	40.85%	31.38%	36.67%
SVM	69.94%	23.36%	16.28%	11.36%

Table 8: WER and DER for Lexicon Retrieval and Statistical SVM techniques for including and excluding case ending

Table 8 shows that excluding case ending (letter) from the evaluation gives better results in terms of WER and DER.

As shown in Table 9, it is noted that including the case ending technique has enhanced dramatically the results of diacritic restoration. Further enhancement was obtained by adopting a new method to restore internal diacritics, when all of the hybrid techniques fail to return any solution; the new method, we call it "accepts any" (AA),

[6] Results for "Excluding CE" are calculated manually for a limited number of test files because Case-Ending diacritic is not always at the last character.

is used for arbitrary accepting results from lexicon.

Technique	WER	DER
LR+DB	35.81%	9.77%
LR+DB+SVM	33.51%	7.99%
LR+DB+SVM+CE	**17.31%**	**4.41%**
LR+DB+SVM+CE+AA	16.66%	3.84%

Table 9: WER and DER for different combination of diacritization techniques

To investigate the effect of enhancing POS tagging on the internal SVM statistical technique, we adapted our modules to interact with ArabicSVMTools, the up-to-date most famous free tagger[7]. Some modification were made to our module to accept the article 'Al' as it may occur as radical letters inside the Noun (we handle 'Al' separately in our tokenizer). We evaluated our statistical diacritization approach using ArabicSVMTools and our proposed tagger. The use of ArabicSVMTools has improved the performance of our diacrtizer as shown in Table 10. ArabicSVMTools gave better results than our proposed tagger. However, our proposed tagger is about 4 times faster than ArabicSVMTools because we use less features.

Tagger	WER	DER
ArabicSVMTools	12.79%	9.94%
Proposed SVM	16.28%	11.36%

Table 10: WER and DER for statistical approach using different taggers without considering case-ending diacritics.

Table 11, shows the results after modifying both the statistical and the case ending approaches for TOK2, POS2, and CE2 tasks. The last row represent results after adding some simple heuristic rules (SHR) to correctly add Tanween Kasra instead of Tanween el Fatha in case of sound plural feminine "جمع المؤنث السالم".

Technique	WER	DER
LR+DB+SVM	31.86%	7.92%
LS+DB+SVM+CE	**12.16%**	**3.78%**
LS+DB+SVM+CE+SHR	11.795%	3.245%

Table 11: WER and DER for different techniques

[7] ArabicSVMTools: http://www.cs.columbia.edu/~mdiab/downloads/ArabicSVMTools.tar.gz

6 Conclusions and Future work

In this paper, we proposed a diacritization model that distinguishes between internal and case ending diacritization. The overall performance is comparable with the best diacritization model that was reported in the literature so far.

Statistically based methods show great promise in addressing the ambiguity resolution problem in Arabic language diacritization.

The proposed system yields good results in the DER and WER compared with MADA-D system, the modifications for case ending algorithm have enhanced the performance.

The proposed system has an advantage that we can use all internal diacritics approaches in parallel because there is no such dependency between algorithms. Nevertheless, the case ending algorithm can also be processed in parallel with the statistical approach. Such parallel processing advantage can improve the response time that could be critical for some diacritization-based real time systems.

Maintaining the bigram database up-to-date will significantly enhance the performance of the system.

Our future work will include adding some heuristic rules for the proposed model as a post processing. This will enhance the performance for the system especially to restore correct diacritics of the possessive personal pronounce suffixes "نا"،"ه". Moreover, adding extra POS tag sets to distinguish between dual noun and plural nouns will enhance the diacritization results. We plan also to enrich the system by increasing the training set by using latest fully diacritized Treebank like Part1 V3.0 (Maamouri et al, 2008) which is not available due to limitation of our budget. This has the effect of enhancing the system performance and allow us to make a comparison with other systems, such as (Habash and Rambow, 2007) and (Zitouni et al. , 2006) .

References

Abo Bakr H. M. , Shaalan K., Ziedan I., 2008, "A Statistical Method for Adding Case Ending Diacritics for Arabic Text", The Eighth Conference on Language Engineering, ESOLEC'2008, Page 225-234, Cairo, Egypt,Deceber 17-18 2008.

Ananthakrishnan, Narayanan S., and Bangalore S., (2005), "Automatic diacritization of arabic transcripts for asr". In Proceedings of ICON-05, Kanpur, India.

Buckwalter T., (2002). Buckwalter Arabic morphological analyzer version 1.0. Technical report, Lin-

guistic Data Consortium, LDC2002L49 and ISBN 1-58563-257-0.
Cristianini N. and Taylor J.S., (2000), "An Introduction to Support Vector Machines and Other Kernel-based Learning Methods", The Press Syndicate of the University of Cambridge, Cambridge, United Kingdom.
Diab M., Hacioglu K., and Jurafsky D., (2004), "Automatic Tagging of Arabic Text: From Raw Text to Base Phrase Chunks," In Proc. of HLT/NAACL 2004, Boston.
Diab M., Hacioglu K., and Jurafsky D.,(2007), "Arabic Computational Morphology Knowledge-based and Empirical Methods" - Chapter 7 "Automatic Processing of Modern Standard Arabic Text",ISBN: 978-1-4020-6046-5, SpringerLink.
El-Imam Y., (2003). Phonetization of Arabic: rules and algorithms. Computer Speech and Language, 18:339–373.
El-Sadany T. and Hashish M., (1988). Semi-automatic vowelization of Arabic verbs. In 10th NC Conference, Jeddah, Saudi Arabia.
Elshafei M., Al-Muhtaseb H., and Alghamdi M., (2006), "Statistical Methods for Automatic Diacritization of Arabic Text". The Saudi 18th National Computer Conference. Riyadh. 18: 301-306.
Emam O. and Fisher V. (2004)., A hierarchical approach for the statistical vowelization of Arabic text. Technical report, IBM patent filed, DE9-2004-0006, US patent application US2005/0192809 A1.
Gal Y., (2002). An HMM approach to vowel restoration in Arabic and Hebrew. In ACL-02 Workshop on Computational Approaches to Semitic Languages.
Habash N. and Rambow O., (2007), "Arabic Diacritization through Full Morphological Tagging", In Proceedings of the North American chapter of the Association for Computational Linguistics (NAACL), Rochester, New York.
Hearst M. A., (1998), "Support Vector Machines," IEEE Intelligent Systems, vol. 13, no. 4, pp. 18-28, Jul/Aug, 1998.
Kirchhoff K. and Vergyri D., (2005). Cross-dialectal data sharing for acoustic modeling in Arabic speech recognition. Speech Communication, 46(1):37–51, May.
Kudo T. and Matsumoto Y., (2003), " Fast methods for kernel-based text analysis," In Proceedings of the 41st Annual Meeting on Association For Computational Linguistics - Volume 1 (Sapporo, Japan, July 07 - 12, 2003). Annual Meeting of the ACL. Association for Computational Linguistics, Morristown.
Maamouri, M., Bies, A. & Buckwalter, T. (2004). The Penn Arabic treebank: Building a largescale annotated Arabic corpus. In NEMLAR Conference on Arabic Language Resources and Tools, Cairo, Egypt.
Maamouri M., Bies A., Kulick S., (2008), "Enhanced Annotation and Parsing of the Arabic Treebank"; INFOS 2008, Cairo, Egypt, March 27-29, 2008.
Sang E. and Buchholz S., (2000), " Introduction to the CoNLL-2000 Shared Task: Chunking", Proceeding of CoNLL-2000 and LLL-2000,Page 127-132, Lisbon,Portugal.
Zitouni I., Sorensen J. S., and Sarikaya R., (2006), "Maximum entropy based restoration of Arabic diacritics". In Proceedings of ACL'06.

Unsupervised Concept Discovery In Hebrew Using Simple Unsupervised Word Prefix Segmentation for Hebrew and Arabic

Elad Dinur[1] **Dmitry Davidov**[2] **Ari Rappoport**[1]

[1]Institute of Computer Science
[2]ICNC
The Hebrew University of Jerusalem

Abstract

Fully unsupervised pattern-based methods for discovery of word categories have been proven to be useful in several languages. The majority of these methods rely on the existence of function words as separate text units. However, in morphology-rich languages, in particular Semitic languages such as Hebrew and Arabic, the equivalents of such function words are usually written as morphemes attached as prefixes to other words. As a result, they are missed by word-based pattern discovery methods, causing many useful patterns to be undetected and a drastic deterioration in performance. To enable high quality lexical category acquisition, we propose a simple unsupervised word segmentation algorithm that separates these morphemes. We study the performance of the algorithm for Hebrew and Arabic, and show that it indeed improves a state-of-art unsupervised concept acquisition algorithm in Hebrew.

1 Introduction

In many NLP tasks, we wish to extract information or perform processing on text using minimal knowledge on the input natural language. Towards this goal, we sometimes find it useful to divide the set of words in natural language to function words and content words, a division that applies in the vast majority of languages. Function words (or grammatical words, e.g., a, an, the, in, of, etc) are words that have little or highly ambiguous lexical meaning, and serve to express grammatical or semantic relationships with the other words in a sentence.

In some morphologically-rich languages, important function words are not written as space-separated units but as morphemes attached as prefixes to other words. This fact can cause problems when statistically analyzing text in these languages, for two main reasons: (1) the vocabulary of the language grows, as our lexical knowledge comes solely from a corpus (words appear with and without the function morphemes); (2) information derived from the presence of these morphemes in the sentence is usually lost.

In this paper we address the important task of a fully unsupervised acquisition of Hebrew lexical categories (or concepts – words sharing a significant aspect of their meaning). We are not aware of any previous work on this task for Hebrew. Due to the problem above, the performance of many acquisition algorithms deteriorates unacceptably. This happens, for example, in the (Davidov and Rappoport, 2006) algorithm that utilizes automatically detected function words as the main building block for pattern construction.

In order to overcome this problem, one should separate such prefixes from the compound words (words consisting of function morphemes attached to content words) in the input corpus. When we consider some particular word, there are frequently many options to split it to smaller strings. Fortunately, the set of function words is small and closed, and the set of grammatical sequences of function prefixes is also small. Hence we assume it does not cost us much to know in advance what are the possible sequences for a specific language.

Even when considering the small number of possible function words, the task of separating them is not simple, as some words may be ambiguous. When reading a word that starts with a prefix known to be a function morpheme, the word may

Proceedings of the EACL 2009 Workshop on Computational Approaches to Semitic Languages, pages 36–44,
Athens, Greece, 31 March, 2009.

be a compound word, or it may be a meaningful word by itself. For example, the word "hsws" in Hebrew[1] can be interpreted as "hsws" (hesitation), or "h sws" (the horse). The segmentation of the word is context dependent – the same string may be segmented differently in different contexts.

One way of doing such word prefix segmentation is to perform a complete morphological disambiguation of the sentence. The disambiguation algorithm finds for each word its morphological attributes (POS tag, gender, etc.), and decides whether a word is a compound word or a word without prefixes. A disambiguation algorithm generally relies on a language-specific morphological analyzer. It may also require a large manually tagged corpus, construction of which for some particular language or domain requires substantial human labor. We avoid the utilization of such costly and language-specific disambiguation algorithms and manually annotated data.

In this paper we present a novel method to separate function word prefixes, and evaluate it using manually labeled gold standards in Hebrew and Arabic. We incorporate the method into a pattern-based Hebrew concept acquisition framework and show that it greatly improves state-of-art results for unsupervised lexical category acquisition. This improvement allows the pattern-based unsupervised framework to use one-tenth of the Hebrew data in order to reach a similar level of results.

Section 2 discusses related work, and Section 3 reviews the word categories discovery algorithm. Section 4 presents the word prefix segmentation algorithm. Results are given in Section 5.

2 Related Work

In this paper we develop an unsupervised framework for segmentation of the function words for languages where context is important for correct segmentation. Our main target language is Hebrew, and we experimented with Arabic as well. As far as we know, there is no work on unsupervised segmentation of words in Hebrew which does not utilize language-specific tools such as morphological analyzers.

Lee et al. (2003) addressed supervised word segmentation in Arabic and have some aspects similar to our approach. As in their study, we also have a pre-supplied list of possible prefix sequences and assume a trigram model in order to find the most probable morpheme sequence. Both studies evaluate performance on a segmented text, and not just on words in the lexicon. However, their algorithm, while achieving good performance (97% accuracy), relies on a training set – a manually segmented corpus of about 110,000 words, while our unsupervised framework does not require any annotation and is thus easier to implement and to apply to different domains and languages.

Snyder and Barzilay (2008) study the task of unsupervised morphological segmentation of multiple languages. Their algorithm automatically induces a segmentation and morpheme alignment of short parallel phrases from a multilingual corpus. Their corpus (The Hebrew Bible and translations) contains parallel phrases in English, Arabic, Hebrew and Aramaic. They obtain 63.87 F-Score for Hebrew words segmentation (prefix and suffix), where recall and precision is calculated based on all possible segmentation points.

Another type of segmentation algorithms involves utilization of language-specific morphological analyzers for complete morphological disambiguation. In Hebrew each word usually has more than one possible POS (along with other attributes, such as gender, number, etc.). Assuming we have a morphological analyzer (producing the set of possible analyses for a given word), we can try to discover the correct segmentation of each word.

Levinger et al. (1995) developed a method for disambiguation of the results provided by a morphological analyzer for Hebrew. Adler and Elhadad (2006) proposed an unsupervised algorithm for word segmentation. They estimate an initial language model (using (Levinger et al., 1995)) and improve this model with EM. Direct comparison to their work is problematic, however, since we avoid utilization of a language-specific morphology/POS analyzer. There are also studies of this type that utilize labeled data (Bar-Haim et al., 2005), where the language model is learned from the training data.

Extensive research has been done on word segmentation, where, unlike in our study, the segmentation is evaluated for every *word*, regardless of its context. Creutz (2003) presents an algorithm for unsupervised segmentation under these assumptions. He proposes a probabilistic model which

[1]Transcription is according to (Ornan, 2005), except for Shin which is denoted by "$".

utilizes the distributions of morpheme length and frequency to estimate the quality of the induced morphemes. Dasgupta and Ng (2007) improves over (Creutz, 2003) by suggesting a simpler approach. They segment a prefix using the word frequency with and without a prefix. Other recent studies that follow the context-independent setup include (Creutz and Lagus, 2005; Keshava and Pitler, 2005; Demberg, 2007). They test their methods on English, Finnish and Turkish. All of these studies, however, assume context-independency of segmentation, disregarding the ambiguity that may come from context. This makes it problematic to apply the proposed methods to context-dependent morphology types as in Hebrew and Arabic.

The guiding goal in the present paper is the concept acquisition problem. Concept acquisition of different kinds has been studied extensively. The two main classification axes for this task are the type of human input and annotation, and the basic algorithmic approach used. The two main algorithmic approaches are clustering of context feature vectors and pattern-based discovery.

The first approach is to map each word to a feature vector and cluster these vectors. Example of such algorithms are (Pereira et al., 1993) and (Lin, 1998) that use syntactic features in the vector definition. Pantel and Lin (2002) improves on the latter by clustering by committee.

Recently, there is a growing interest in the second main algorithmic approach, usage of lexico-syntactic patterns. Patterns have been shown to produce more accurate results than feature vectors, at a lower computational cost on large corpora (Pantel et al., 2004). Thus (Dorow et al., 2005) discover categories using two basic pre-specified patterns ("x and y", "x or y").

Some recent studies have proposed frameworks that attempt to avoid any implicit or explicit pre-specification of patterns. Davidov and Rappoport (2006) proposed a method that detects function words by their high frequency, and utilizes these words for the discovery of symmetric patterns. Their method is based on two assumptions: (1) some function words in the language symmetrically connect words belonging to the same category; (2) such function words can be detected as the most frequent words in language. While these assumptions are reasonable for many languages, for some morphologically rich languages the second assumption may fail. This is due to the fact that some languages like Hebrew and Arabic may express relationships not by isolated function words but by morphemes attached in writing to other words.

As an example, consider the English word "and', which was shown to be very useful in concept acquisition (Dorow et al., 2005). In Hebrew this word is usually expressed as the morpheme "w" attached to the second word in a conjunction ("... *w*sws" – "... and horse"). Patterns discovered by such automatic pattern discovery algorithms are based on isolated words, and hence fail to capture "and"-based relationships that are very useful for detection of words belonging to the same concept. Davidov and Rappoport (2006) reports very good results for English and Russian. However, no previous work applies a fully unsupervised concept acquisition for Hebrew.

In our study we combine their concept acquisition framework with a simple unsupervised word segmentation technique. Our evaluation confirms the weakness of word-based frameworks for morphology-rich languages such as Hebrew, and shows that utilizing the proposed word segmentation can overcome this weakness while keeping the concept acquisition approach fully unsupervised.

3 Unsupervised Discovery of Word Categories

In this study we use word segmentation to improve the (Davidov and Rappoport, 2006) method for discovery of word categories, sets of words sharing a significant aspect of their meaning. An example for such a discovered category is the set of verbs {dive, snorkel, swim, float, surf, sail, drift, ...}. Below we briefly describe this category acquisition algorithm.

The algorithm consists of three stages as follows. First, it discovers a set of pattern candidates, which are defined by a combination of high frequency words (denoted by H) and slots for low frequency (content) words (denoted by C). An example for such a pattern candidate is 'x belongs to y', where 'x' and 'y' stand for content word slots. The patterns are found according to a predefined set of possible meta-patterns. The meta-patterns are language-independent[2] and consist of up to 4

[2]They do not include any specific words, only a relative order of high/low frequency words, and hence can be used on

words in total, from which two are (non-adjacent) content words. Four meta-patterns are used: CHC, CHCH, CHHC, HCHC.

Second, those patterns which give rise to symmetric lexical relationships are identified. The meaning of phrases constructed from those patterns is (almost) invariant to the order of the content words contained in them. An example for such a pattern is 'x and y'. In order to identify such useful patterns, for each pattern we build a graph following (Widdows and Dorow, 2002). The graph is constructed from a node for each content word, and a directed arc from the node 'x' to 'y' if the corresponding content words appear in the pattern such that 'x' precedes 'y'. Then we calculate several symmetry measures on the graph structure and select the patterns with best values for these measures.

The third stage is the generation of categories. We extract tightly connected sets of words from the unified graph which combines all graphs of selected patterns. Such sets of words define the desired categories.

The patterns which include the 'x and y' substring are among the most useful patterns for generation of categories (they were used in (Dorow et al., 2005) and discovered in all 5 languages tested in (Davidov and Rappoport, 2006)). However, in Hebrew such patterns can not be found in the same way, since the function word 'and' is the prefix 'w' and not a standalone high frequency word.

Another popular set of patterns are ones including 'x or y'. Such patterns can be identified in Hebrew, as 'or' in Hebrew is a separate word. However, even in this case, the content word represented by 'x' or 'y' may appear with a prefix. This damages the construction of the pattern graph, since two different nodes may be created instead of one – one for a regular content word, the other for the same word with a prefix. Consequently, it is reasonable to assume that segmenting the corpus in advance should improve the results of discovery of word categories.

4 Word Segmentation Algorithm

We assume we know the small and closed set of grammatical function word prefix sequences in the language[3]. Our input is a sentence, and our objective is to return the correct segmentation of the sentence. A sentence L is a sequence of words $\{w_1, w_2, ..., w_n\}$. A segmentation S_i of L is a sequence of morphemes $\{m_1, m_2, ..., m_k\}$ and $l(S_i)$ is the number of morphemes in the sequence. Note that $l(S_i)$ may be different for each segmentation. The best segmentation S will be calculated by:

$$P(S_i) = p(m_1)p(m_2|m_1)\prod_{i=3}^{l(S_i)} p(m_i|m_{i-1}m_{i-2})$$

$$S = \arg\max_{S_i} P(S_i)$$

Calculation of joint probabilities requires a trigram model of the language. Below we describe the construction of the trigram model and then we detail the algorithm for efficient calculation of S.

4.1 Construction of trigram model

Creating the trigram language model is done in two stages: (1) we segment a corpus automatically, and (2) we learn a trigram language model from the segmented corpus.

4.1.1 Initial corpus segmentation

For initial corpus segmentation, we define a statistical measure for the segmentation of individual words. Let wx be a word, such that w is the prefix of the word composed of a sequence of function word prefixes and x is a string of letters. Let $f(x)$ be the frequency of the word x in the corpus. Denote by al the average length of the strings (with prefixes) in the language. This can be easily estimated from the corpus – every string that appears in the corpus is counted once. $l(x)$ is the number of characters in the word x. We utilize two parameters G, H, where $G < H$ (we used $G = 2.5, H = 3.5$) and define the following functions :

$$factor(x) = \begin{cases} \frac{al-G-l(x)}{al-H} & l(x) < al - G \\ 0 & otherwise \end{cases}$$

$$Rank(wx) = \frac{f(wx)}{f(wx) + f(x)} + factor(x)$$

Note that the expression $\frac{f(wx)}{f(wx)+f(x)}$ is a number in $(0, 1]$, inversely correlated with the frequency of the prefixed word. Thus higher $Rank(wx)$ values indicate that the word is less likely to be composed of the prefix w followed by the word x.

any languages with explicit word segmentation.

[3]Unlike development of labeled training data, handcrafting such a closed set is straightforward for many languages and does not requires any significant time/human labor

The expression $\frac{al-G-l(x)}{al-H}$ is a number in $(0,1]$, therefore $factor(x) \in [0,1]$. H is $G-1$ in order to keep the expression smaller than 1. The term $factor(x)$ is greater as x is shorter. The factor is meant to express the fact that short words are less likely to have a prefix. We have examined this in Hebrew – as there are no words of length 1, two letter words have no prefix. We have analyzed 102 randomly chosen three letter words, and found that only 19 of them were prefixed words. We have analyzed 100 randomly chosen four letter words, and found that 40 of them were prefixed words. The result was about the same for five letter words. In order to decide whether a word needs to be separated, we define a threshold $T \in [0,1]$. We allow word separation only when $Rank(wx)$ is lower than T. When there are more than two possible sequences of function word prefixes ("$mhsws$","$m\ hsws$", "$mh\ sws$"), we choose the segmentation with the lower rank.

4.1.2 Learning the trigram model

The learning of the language model is based on counts of the corpus, assigning a special symbol, "u/k" (unknown) for all words that do not appear in the corpus. As estimated by (Lee et al., 2003), we set the probability of "u/k" to be $1E-9$. The value of the symbol "u/k" was observed to be significant. We found that the value proposed by (Lee et al., 2003) for Arabic gives good results also for Hebrew.

4.2 Dynamic programming approach for word segmentation

The naive method to find S is to iterate over all possible segmentations of the sentence. This method may fail to handle long sentences, as the number of segmentations grows exponentially with the length of the sentence. To overcome this problem, we use dynamic programming.

Each morpheme has an index i to its place in a segmentation sequence. Iteratively, for index i, for every morpheme which appears in some segmentation in index i, we calculate the best segmentation of the sequence $m_1 \ldots m_i$. Two problems arise here: (1) we need to calculate which morphemes may appear in a given index; (2) we need to constrain the calculation, such that only valid segmentations would be considered.

To calculate which morphemes can appear in a given index we define the object *Morpheme*. It contains the morpheme (string), the index of a word in the sentence the morpheme belongs to, reference to the preceding *Morpheme* in the same word, and indication whether it is the last morpheme in the word. For each index of the sentence segmentation, we create a list of *Morphemes* (index-list).

For each word w_i, and for segmentation $m_i^1, .., m_i^k$, we create *Morphemes* $M_i^1, .., M_i^k$. We traverse sequentially the words in the sentence, and for each segmentation we add the sequence of *Morphemes* to all possible index-lists. The index-list for the first *Morpheme* M_i^1 is the combination of successors of all the index-lists that contain a *Morpheme* M_{i-1}^k. The constraints are enforced easily – if a *Morpheme* M_i^j is the first in a word, the preceding *Morpheme* in the sequence must be the last *Morpheme* of the previous word. Otherwise, the preceding *Morpheme* must be M_i^{j-1}, which is referenced by M_i^j.

4.3 Limitations

While our model handles the majority of cases, it does not fully comply with a linguistic analysis of Hebrew, as there are a few minor exceptions. We assumed that there is no ambiguity in the function word prefixes. This is not entirely correct, as in Hebrew we have two different kinds of exceptions for this rule. For example, the prefix "k$" (when), can also be interpreted as the prefix "k" (as) followed by the prefix "$" (that). As the second interpretation is rare, we always assumed it is the prefix "k$". This rule was applied wherever an ambiguity exists. However, we did not treat this problem as it is very rare, and in the development set and test set it did not appear even once.

A harder problem is encountered when processing the word "bbyt". Two interpretations could be considered here: "b byt" ("in a house"), and "b h byt" ("in the house"). Whether this actually poses a problem or not depends on the application. We assume that the correct segmentation here is "b byt". Without any additional linguistic knowledge (for example, diacritical vowel symbols should suffice in Hebrew), solving these problems requires some prior discriminative data.

5 Evaluation and Results

We evaluate our algorithm in two stages. First we test the quality of our unsupervised word segmentation framework on Hebrew and Arabic, comparing our segmentation results to a manually anno-

	With $factor(x)$				Without $factor(x)$			
T	Prec.	Recall	F-Measure	Accuracy	Prec.	Recall	F-Measure	Accuracy
0.70	0.844	0.798	0.820	0.875	0.811	0.851	0.830	0.881
0.73	0.841	0.828	0.834	0.883	0.808	0.866	0.836	0.884
0.76	0.837	0.846	0.841	0.886	0.806	0.882	0.842	0.887
0.79	**0.834**	**0.870**	**0.851**	**0.893**	0.803	0.897	0.847	0.890
0.82	0.826	0.881	0.852	0.892	0.795	0.904	0.846	0.888
0.85	0.820	0.893	0.854	0.892	0.787	0.911	0.844	0.886
0.88	0.811	0.904	0.855	0.891	0.778	0.917	0.841	0.882

Table 1: Ranks vs. Threshold T for Hebrew.

	With $factor(x)$				Without $factor(x)$			
T	Prec.	Recall	F-Measure	Accuracy	Prec.	Recall	F-Measure	Accuracy
0.91	0.940	0.771	0.846	0.892	0.903	0.803	0.850	0.891
0.93	0.930	0.797	0.858	0.898	0.903	0.840	0.870	0.904
0.95	0.931	0.810	0.866	0.904	0.902	0.856	0.878	0.909
0.97	0.927	0.823	0.872	0.906	0.896	0.869	0.882	0.911
0.99	0.925	0.848	0.872	0.915	0.878	0.896	0.886	0.913
1.00	**0.923**	**0.852**	**0.886**	**0.915**	0.841	0.896	0.867	0.895

Table 2: Ranks vs. Threshold T for Arabic.

Algorithm	P	R	F	A
Rank seg.	**0.834**	**0.870**	**0.851**	**0.893**
Baseline	0.561	0.491	0.523	0.69
Morfessor	0.630	0.689	0.658	0.814

Table 3: Segmentation results comparison.

tated gold standard. Then we incorporate word segmentation into a concept acquisition framework and compare the performance of this framework with and without word segmentation.

5.1 Corpora and annotation

For our experiments in Hebrew we used a 19MB Hebrew corpus obtained from the "Mila" Knowledge Center for Processing Hebrew[4]. The corpus consists of 143,689 different words, and a total of 1,512,737 word tokens. A sample text of size about 24,000 words was taken from the corpus, manually segmented by human annotators and used as a gold standard in our segmentation evaluation. In order to estimate the quality of our algorithm for Arabic, we used a 7MB Arabic news items corpus, and a similarly manually annotated test text of 4715 words. The Arabic corpus is too small for meaningful category discovery, so we used it only in the segmentation evaluation.

5.2 Evaluation of segmentation framework

In order to estimate the performance of word segmentation as a standalone algorithm we applied our algorithm on the Hebrew and Arabic corpora, using different parameter settings. We first calculated the word frequencies, then applied initial segmentation as described in Section 4. Then we used SRILM (Stolcke, 2002) to learn the trigram model from the segmented corpus. We utilized Good-Turing discounting with Katz backoff, and we gave words that were not in the training set the constant probability $1E-9$. Finally we utilized the obtained trigram model to select sentence segmentations. To test the influence of the $factor(x)$ component of the $Rank$ value, we repeated our experiment with and without usage of this component. We also ran our algorithm with a set of different threshold T values in order to study the influence of this parameter.

Tables 1 and 2 show the obtained results for Hebrew and Arabic respectively. Precision is the ratio of correct prefixes to the total number of detected prefixes in the text. Recall is the ratio of prefixes that were split correctly to the total number of prefixes. Accuracy is the number of correctly segmented words divided by the total number of words.

As can be seen from the results, the best F-score with and without usage of the $factor(x)$ component are about the same, but usage of this component gives higher precision for the same F-score. From comparison of Arabic and Hebrew performance we can also see that segmentation decisions for the task in Arabic are likely to be easier, since the accuracy for T=1 is very high. It means that, unlike in Hebrew (where the best results were obtained for T=0.79), a word which starts with a pre-

[4] http://mila.cs.technion.ac.il.

Method	us	k-means	random
avg 'shared meaning'(%)	**85**	24.61	10
avg triplet score(1-4)	**1.57**	2.32	3.71
avg category score(1-10)	**9.35**	6.62	3.5

Table 4: Human evaluation results.

abuse, robbery, murder, assault, extortion
good, cheap, beautiful, comfortable
son, daughter, brother, parent
when, how, where
essential, important, central, urgent

Table 5: A sample from the lexical categories discovered in Hebrew (translated to English).

fix should generally be segmented.

We also compared our best results to the baseline and to previous work. The baseline draws a segmentation uniformly for each word, from the possible segmentations of the word. In an attempt to partially reproduce (Creutz and Lagus, 2005) on our data, we also compared our results to the results obtained from Morfessor Categories-MAP, version 0.9.1 (Described in (Creutz and Lagus, 2005)). The Morfessor Categories-MAP algorithm gets a list of words and their frequencies, and returns the segmentation for every word. Since Morfessor may segment words with prefixes which do not exist in our predefined list of valid prefixes, we did not segment the words that had illegal prefixes as segmented by Morfessor.

Results for this comparison are shown in Table 3. Our method significantly outperforms both the baseline and Morfessor-based segmentation. We have also tried to improve the language model by a self training scheme on the same corpus but we observed only a slight improvement, giving 0.848 Precision and 0.872 Recall.

5.3 Discovery of word categories

We divide the evaluation of the word categories discovery into two parts. The first is evaluating the improvement in the quantity of found lexical categories. The second is evaluating the quality of these categories. We have applied the algorithm to a Hebrew corpus of size 130MB[5], which is sufficient for a proof of concept. We compared the output of the categories discovery on two different settings, with function word separation and without such separation. In both settings we omitted all punctuation symbols. In both runs of the algorithm we used the same parameters. Eight symmetric patterns were automatically chosen for each run. Two of the patterns that were chosen by the algorithm in the unseparated case were also chosen in the separated case.

[5]Again obtained from the "Mila" Knowledge Center for Processing Hebrew.

	N	A	J
With Separation	148	4.1	1
No Separation	36	2.9	0

Table 6: Lexical categories discovery results comparison. N: number of categories. A: average category size. J: 'junk' words.

5.3.1 Manual estimation of category quality

Evaluating category quality is challenging since no exhaustive lists or gold standards are widely accepted even in English, certainly so in resource-poor languages such as Hebrew. Hence we follow the human judgment evaluation scheme presented in (Davidov and Rappoport, 2006), for the categories obtained from the segmented corpus.

We compared three methods of word categories discovery. The first is random sampling of words into categories. The second is k-means, where each word is mapped to a vector, and similarity is calculated as described in (Pantel and Lin, 2002). We applied k-means to the set of vectors, with similarity as a distance function. If a vector had low similarity with all means, we leave it unattached. Therefore some clusters contained only one vector. Running the algorithm 10 times, with different initial means each time, produced 60 clusters with three or more words. An interesting phenomenon we observed is that this method produces very nice clusters of named entities. The last method is the one in (Davidov and Rappoport, 2006).

The experiment contained two parts. In Part I, subjects were given 40 triplets of words and were asked to rank them using the following scale: (1) the words definitely share a significant part of their meaning; (2) the words have a shared meaning but only in some context; (3) the words have a shared meaning only under a very unusual context/situation; (4) the words do not share any meaning; (5) I am not familiar enough with some/all of the words.

The 40 triplets were obtained as follows. 20 of our categories were selected at random from the non-overlapping categories we have discovered, and three words were selected from each of these at random. 10 triplets were selected in the same manner from the categories produced by k-means, and 10 triplets were selected at random from content words in the same document.

In Part II, subjects were given the full categories represented by the triplets that were graded as 1 or 2 in Part I (the full "good" categories in terms of sharing of meaning). Subjects were asked to grade the categories from 1 (worst) to 10 (best) according to how much the full category had met the expectations they had when seeing only the triplet.

Nine people participated in the evaluation. A summary of the results is given in Table 4.

The categories obtained from the unsegmented corpus are too few and too small for a significant evaluation. Therefore we applied the evaluation scheme only for the segmented corpus.

The results from the segmented corpus contain some interesting categories, with a 100% precision, like colors, Arab leaders, family members and cities. An interesting category is {Arabic, English, Russian, French, German, Yiddish, Polish, Math}. A sample of some other interesting categories can be seen in Table 5.

5.3.2 Segmentation effect on category discovery

In Table 6, we find that there is a major improvement in the number of acquired categories, and an interesting improvement in the average category size. One might expect that as a consequence of an incorrect segmentation of a word, "junk" words may appear in the discovered categories. As can be seen, only one "junk" word was categorized.

Throughout this paper we have assumed that function word properties of languages such as Hebrew and Arabic decrease performance of whole-word pattern-based concept acquisition methods. To check this assumption, we have applied the concept acquisition algorithm on several web-based corpora of several languages, while choosing corpora size to be exactly equal to the size of the Hebrew corpus (130Mb) and utilizing exactly the same parameters. We did not perform quality evaluation[6], but measured the number of concepts and concept size. Indeed the number of categories was (190, 170, 159, 162, 150, 29) for Russian, English, Spanish, French, Turkish and Arabic respectively, clearly inferior for Arabic in comparison to these European and Slavic languages. A similar tendency was observed for average concept size. At the same time prefix separation does help to extract 148 concepts for Hebrew, making it nearly inline with other languages. In contrast, our preliminary experiments on English and Russian suggest that the effect of applying similar morphological segmentation on these languages in insignificant.

In order to test whether more data can substitute segmentation even for Hebrew, we have obtained by means of crawling and web queries a larger (while potentially much more noisy) web-based 2GB Hebrew corpus which is based on forum and news contents. Our goal was to estimate which unsegmented corpus size (if any) can bring similar performance (in terms of concept number, size and quality). We gradually increased corpus size and applied the concept acquisition algorithm on this corpus. Finally, we have obtained similar, nearly matching, results to our 130MB corpus for a 1.2GB Hebrew subcorpus of the 2GB Hebrew corpus. The results remain stable for 4 different 1.2GB subsets taken from the same 2GB corpus. This suggests that while segmentation can be substituted with more data, it may take roughly x10 more data for Hebrew to obtain the same results without segmentation as with it.

[6]Brief manual examination suggests no significant drops in concept quality.

6 Summary

We presented a simple method for separating function word prefixes from words. The method requires very little language-specific knowledge (the prefixes), and it can be applied to any morphologically rich language. We showed that this segmentation dramatically improves lexical acquisition in Hebrew, where nearly $\times 10$ data is required to obtain the same number of concepts without segmentation.

While in this paper we evaluated our framework on the discovery of concepts, we have recently proposed fully unsupervised frameworks for the discovery of different relationship types (Davidov et al., 2007; Davidov and Rappoport, 2008a; Davidov and Rappoport, 2008b). Many of these methods are mostly based on function words, and may greatly benefit from the proposed segmentation framework.

References

Meni Adler, Michael Elhadad, 2006. An Unsupervised Morpheme-Based HMM for Hebrew Morphological Disambiguation. *ACL '06.*

Roy Bar-Haim, Khalil Simaan, Yoad Winter, 2005. Choosing an Optimal Architecture for Segmentation and POS-Tagging of Modern Hebrew. *ACL Workshop on Computational Approaches to Semitic Languages '05.*

Mathias Creutz, 2003. Unsupervised Segmentation of Words Using Prior Distributions of Morph Length and Frequency. *ACL '03.*

Mathias Creutz and Krista Lagus, 2005. Unsupervised Morpheme Segmentation and Morphology Induction from Text Corpora Using Morfessor 1.0. *In Computer and Information Science, Report A81, Helsinki University of Technology.*

Sajib Dasgupta and Vincent Ng, 2007. High Performance, Language-Independent Morphological Segmentation. *NAACL/HLT '07.*

Dmitry Davidov, Ari Rappoport, 2006. Efficient Unsupervised Discovery of Word Categories Using Symmetric Patterns and High Frequency Words. *ACL '06.*

Dmitry Davidov, Ari Rappoport, Moshe Koppel, 2007. Fully Unsupervised Discovery of Concept-Specific Relationships by Web Mining. *ACL '07.*

Dmitry Davidov, Ari Rappoport, 2008a. Classification of Semantic Relationships between Nominals Using Pattern Clusters. *ACL '08.*

Dmitry Davidov, Ari Rappoport, 2008b. Unsupervised Discovery of Generic Relationships Using Pattern Clusters and its Evaluation by Automatically Generated SAT Analogy Questions. *ACL '08.*

Vera Demberg, 2007. A Language-Independent Unsupervised Model for Morphological Segmentation. *ACL '07.*

Beate Dorow, Dominic Widdows, Katarina Ling, Jean-Pierre Eckmann, Danilo Sergi, Elisha Moses, 2005. Using Curvature and Markov Clustering in Graphs for Lexical Acquisition and Word Sense Discrimination. *MEANING '05.*

Samarth Keshava, Emily Pitler, 2006. A Simpler, Intuitive Approach to Morpheme Induction. *In Proceedings of 2nd Pascal Challenges Workshop, Venice, Italy.*

Young-Suk Lee, Kishore Papineni, Salim Roukos, Ossama Emam, Hany Hassan, 2003. Language Model Based Arabic Word Segmentation. *ACL '03.*

Moshe Levinger, Uzzi Ornan, Alon Itai, 1995. Learning Morpho-Lexical Probabilities from an Untagged Corpus with an Application to Hebrew. *Comput. Linguistics, 21:383:404.*

Dekang Lin, 1998. Automatic Retrieval and Clustering of Similar Words. *COLING '98.*

Uzzi Ornan, 2005. Hebrew in Latin Script. *Lesonenu, LXIV:137:151 (in Hebrew).*

Patrick Pantel, Dekang Lin, 2002. Discovering Word Senses from Text. *SIGKDD '02.*

Patrick Pantel, Deepak Ravichandran, Eduard Hovy, 2004. Towards Terascale Knowledge Acquisition. *COLING '04.*

Fernando Pereira, Naftali Tishby, Lillian Lee, 1993. Distributional Clustering of English Words. *ACL '93.*

Benjamin Snyder, Regina Bazilay, 2008. Unsupervised Multilingual Learning for Morphological Segmentation. *ACL/HLT '08.*

Andreas Stolcke, 2002. SRILM – an Extensible Language Modeling Toolkit. *ICSLP, pages 901-904, Denver, Colorado.*

Dominic Widdows, Beate Dorow, 2002. A Graph Model for Unsupervised Lexical Acquisition. *COLING '02.*

Automatic Treebank-Based Acquisition of Arabic LFG Dependency Structures

Lamia Tounsi **Mohammed Attia** **Josef van Genabith**

NCLT, School of Computing, Dublin City University, Ireland
{lamia.tounsi, mattia, josef}@computing.dcu.ie

Abstract

A number of papers have reported on methods for the automatic acquisition of large-scale, probabilistic LFG-based grammatical resources from treebanks for English (Cahill and al., 2002), (Cahill and al., 2004), German (Cahill and al., 2003), Chinese (Burke, 2004), (Guo and al., 2007), Spanish (O'Donovan, 2004), (Chrupala and van Genabith, 2006) and French (Schluter and van Genabith, 2008). Here, we extend the LFG grammar acquisition approach to Arabic and the Penn Arabic Treebank (ATB) (Maamouri and Bies, 2004), adapting and extending the methodology of (Cahill and al., 2004) originally developed for English. Arabic is challenging because of its morphological richness and syntactic complexity. Currently 98% of ATB trees (without FRAG and X) produce a covering and connected f-structure. We conduct a qualitative evaluation of our annotation against a gold standard and achieve an f-score of 95%.

1 Introduction

Treebank-based statistical parsers tend to achieve greater coverage and robustness compared to approaches using handcrafted grammars. However, they are criticised for being too shallow to mark important syntactic and semantic dependencies needed for meaning-sensitive applications (Kaplan, 2004). To treat this deficiency, a number of researchers have concentrated on enriching shallow parsers with deep dependency information. (Cahill and al., 2002), (Cahill and al., 2004) outlined an approach which exploits information encoded in the Penn-II Treebank (PTB) trees to automatically annotate each node in each tree with LFG f-structure equations representing deep predicate-argument structure relations. From this LFG annotated treebank, large-scale unification grammar resources were automatically extracted and used in parsing (Cahill and al., 2008) and generation (Cahill and van Genabith, 2006). This approach was subsequently extended to other languages including German (Cahill and al., 2003), Chinese (Burke, 2004), (Guo and al., 2007), Spanish (O'Donovan, 2004), (Chrupala and van Genabith, 2006) and French (Schluter and van Genabith, 2008).

Arabic is a semitic language and is well-known for its morphological richness and syntactic complexity. In this paper we describe the porting of the LFG annotation methodology to Arabic in order to induce LFG f-structures from the Penn Arabic Treebank (ATB) (Bies, 2003), (Maamouri and Bies, 2004). We evaluate both the coverage and quality of the automatic f-structure annotation of the ATB. Ultimately, our goal is to use the f-structure annotated ATB to derive wide-coverage resources for parsing and generating unrestricted Arabic text. In this paper we concentrate on the annotation algorithm.

The paper first provides a brief overview of Lexical Functional Grammar, and the Penn Arabic Treebank (ATB). The next section presents the architecture of the f-structure annotation algorithm for the acquisition of f-structures from the Arabic treebank. The last section provides an evaluation of the quality and coverage of the annotation algorithm.

1.1 Lexical Functional Grammar

Lexical-Functional Grammar (LFG) (Kaplan and Bresnan, 1982); (Bresnan, 2001), (Falk, 2001) 2001, (Sells, 1985) is a constraint-based theory of grammar. LFG rejects concepts of configurationality and movement familiar from generative grammar, and provides a non-derivational alternative of parallel structures of which phrase structure trees are only one component.

LFG involves two basic, parallel forms of

Proceedings of the EACL 2009 Workshop on Computational Approaches to Semitic Languages, pages 45–52,
Athens, Greece, 31 March, 2009.

knowledge representation: c(onstituent)-structure, which is represented by (f-structure annotated) phrase structure trees; and f(unctional)-structure, represented by a matrix of attribute-value pairs. While c-structure accounts for language-specific lexical idiosyncrasies, syntactic surface configurations and word order variations, f-structure provides a more abstract level of representation (grammatical functions/ labeled dependencies), abstracting from some cross-linguistic syntactic differences. Languages may differ typologically as regards surface structural representations, but may still encode similar syntactic functions (such as, subject, object, adjunct, etc.). For a recent overview on LFG-based analyses of Arabic see (Attia, 2008) who presents a hand-crafted Arabic LFG parser using the XLE (Xerox Linguistics Environment).

1.2 The Penn Arabic Treebank (ATB)

The Penn Arabic Treebank project started in 2001 with the aim of describing written Modern Standard Arabic newswire. The Treebank consists of 23611 sentences (Bies, 2003), (Maamouri and Bies, 2004) .

Arabic is a subject pro-drop language: a null category (pro) is allowed in the subject position of a finite clause if the agreement features on the verb are rich enough to enable content to be recovered (Baptista, 1995), (Chomsky, 1981). This is represented in the ATB annotation by an empty node after the verb marked with a -SBJ functional tag. The ATB annotation, following the Penn-II Treebank, utilises the concept of empty nodes and traces to mark long distance dependencies, as in relative clauses and questions.

The default word order in Arabic is VSO. When the subject precedes the verb (SVO), the construction is considered as topicalized. Modern Standard Arabic also allows VOS word order under certain conditions, e.g. when the object is a pronoun. The ATB annotation scheme involves 24 basic POS-tags (497 different tags with morphological information), 22 phrasal tags, and 20 individual functional tags (52 different combined tags).

The relatively free word order of Arabic means that phrase structural position is not an indicator of grammatical function, a feature of English which was heavily exploited in the automatic LFG annotation of the Penn-II Treebank (Cahill and al., 2002). Instead, in the ATB functional tags are used to mark the subject as well as the object.

The syntactic annotation style of the ATB follows, as much as possible, the methodologies and bracketing guidelines already used for the English Penn-II Treebank. For example, in the Penn English Treebank (PTB) (Marcus, 1994), small clauses are considered sentences composed of a subject and a predicate, without traces for an omitted verb or any sort of control relationship, as in example (1) for the sentence "I consider Kris a fool".

```
(1) (S (NP-SBJ I)
        (VP consider
           (S (NP-SBJ Kris)
              (NP-PRD a fool))))
```

The team working on the ATB found this approach very convenient for copula constructions in Arabic, which are mainly verbless (Maamouri and Bies, 2004). Therefore they used a similar analysis without assuming a deleted copula verb or control relationship, as in (2).

```
(2) (S (NP SBJ Al-mas>alatu المسألة)
        (ADJ-PRD basiyTatuN بسيطة))
```

المسألة بسيطة
Al-mas>alatu basiyTatuN
the-question simple
'The question is simple.'

2 Architecture of the Arabic Automatic Annotation Algorithm

The annotation algorithm for Arabic is based on and substantially revises the methodology used for English.

For English, f-structure annotation is very much driven by configurational information: e.g. the leftmost NP sister of a VP is likely to be a direct object and hence annotated $\uparrow$ OBJ $=\downarrow$. This information is captured in the format of left-right annotation matrices, which specify annotations for left or right sisters relative to a local head.

By contrast, Arabic is a lot less configurational and has much richer morphology. In addition, compared to the Penn-II treebank, the ATB features a larger functional tag set. This is reflected in the design of the Arabic f-structure annotation algorithm

(Figure 1), where left-right annotation matrices play a much smaller role than for English. The annotation algorithm recursively traverses trees in the ATB. It exploits ATB morpho-syntactic features, ATB functional tags, and (some) configurational information in the local subtrees.

We first mask (conflate) some of the complex morphological information available in the preterminal nodes to be able to state generalisations for some of the annotation components. We then head-lexicalise ATB trees identifying local heads. Lexical macros exploit the full morphological annotations available in the ATB and map them to corresponding f-structure equations. We then exploit ATB functional tags mapping them to SUBJ, OBJ, OBL, OBJ2, TOPIC and ADJUNCT etc. grammatical functions. The remaining functions (COMP, XCOMP, SPEC etc.) as well as some cases of SUBJ, OBJ, OBL, OBJ2, TOPIC and ADJUNCT, which could not be identified by ATB tags, are treated in terms of left-right context annotation matrices. Coordination is treated in a separate component to keep the other components simple. Catch-all & Clean-Up corrects overgeneralisations in the previous modules and uses defaults for remaining unannotated nodes. Finally, non-local dependencies are handled by a Traces component.

The next sub-sections describe the main modules of the annotation algorithm.

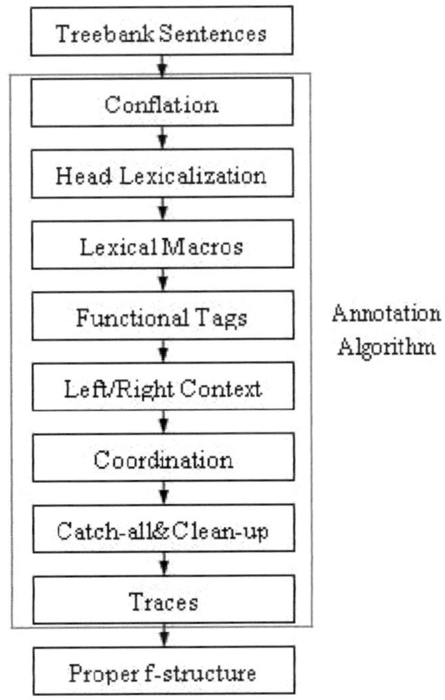

Figure 1: Architecture of the Arabic annotation algorithm

2.1 Conflation

ATB preterminals are very fine-grained, encoding extensive morpho-syntactic details in addition to POS information. For example, the word سنقف `sanaqifu` '[we will] stand' is tagged as (FUT+IV1P+IV+IVSUFF_MOOD:I) denoting an imperfective (I) verb (V) in the future tense (FUT), and is first person (1) plural (P) with indicative mood (IVSUFF_MOOD:I). In total there are over 460 preterminal types in the treebank. This level of fine-grainedness is an important issue for the annotation as we cannot state grammatical function (dependency) generalizations about heads and left and right contexts for such a large tag set. To deal with this problem, for some of the annotation algorithm components we masked the morpho-syntactic details in preterminals, thereby conflating them into more generic POS tags. For example, the above-mentioned tag will be conflated as VERB.

2.2 Lexical Macros

Lexical macros, by contrast, utilise the detailed morpho-syntactic information encoded in the preterminal nodes of the Penn Arabic Treebank trees and provide the required functional annotations accordingly. These tags usually include information related to person, number, gender, definiteness, case, tense, aspect, mood, etc.

Table 1 lists common tags for nouns and verbs and shows the LFG functional annotation assigned to each tag.

2.3 Functional Tags

In addition to monadic POS categories, the ATB treebank contains a set of labels (called functional tags or functional labels) associated with functional information, such as -SBJ for 'subject' and -OBJ for 'object'. The functional tags module translates these functional labels into LFG functional equations, e.g. -OBJ is assigned the annotation $\uparrow$OBJ=$\downarrow$. An f-structure equation look-up table assigns default f-structure equations to each functional label in the ATB (Table 2).

A particular treatment is applied for the tag -PRD (predicate). This functional tag is used with copula complements, as in (3) and the corresponding c-structure in Figure 2. Copula complements

Tag	Annotation
	Nouns
MASC	$\uparrow$ GEND = masc (masculine)
FEM	$\uparrow$ GEND = fem (feminine)
SG	$\uparrow$ NUM = sg (singular)
DU	$\uparrow$ NUM = dual
PL	$\uparrow$ NUM = pl (plural)
ACC	$\uparrow$ CASE = acc (accusative)
NOM	$\uparrow$ CASE = nom (nominative)
GEN	$\uparrow$ CASE = gen (genitive)
	Verbs
1	$\uparrow$ PERS = 1
2	$\uparrow$ PERS = 2
3	$\uparrow$ PERS = 3
S	$\uparrow$ NUM = sg
D	$\uparrow$ NUM = dual
P	$\uparrow$ NUM = pl
F	$\uparrow$ GEND = masc
M	$\uparrow$ GEND = fem

Table 1: Morpho-syntactic tags and their functional annotations

Functional Label	Annotation
-SBJ (subject)	$\uparrow$ SUBJ = $\downarrow$
-OBJ (object)	$\uparrow$ OBJ = $\downarrow$
-DTV (dative), -BNF (Benefactive)	$\uparrow$ OBJ2 =$\downarrow$
-TPC (topicalized)	$\uparrow$ TOPIC=$\downarrow$
-CLR (clearly related)	$\uparrow$ OBL =$\downarrow$
-LOC (locative), -MNR (manner), -DIR (direction), -TMP (temporal), -ADV (adverbial) -PRP (purpose),	$\downarrow\in\uparrow$ ADJUNCT

Table 2: Functional tags used in the ATP Treebank and their default annotations

correspond to the open complement grammatical function XCOMP in LFG and the ATB tag -PRD is associated with the annotation in (4) in order to produce the f-structure in Figure 3. The resulting analysis includes a main predicator 'null_be' and specifies the control relationship through a functional equation stating that the main subject is co-indexed with the subject of the XCOMP.

(3) الهدنة ضروريّة
`Al-hudonapu Daruwriy~apN`
the-truce necessary
'The truce is necessary.'

(4) $\uparrow$ PRED = 'null_be'
$\uparrow$ XCOMP = $\downarrow$
$\uparrow$ SUBJ= $\downarrow$ SUBJ

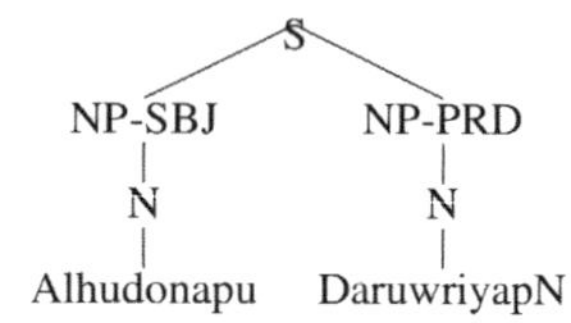

Figure 2: C-structure for example (3)

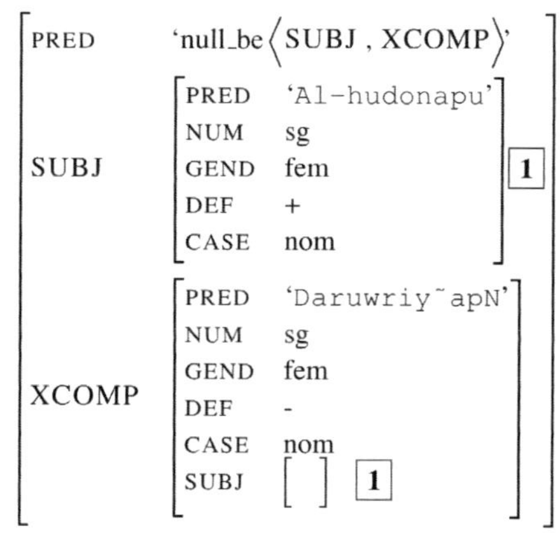

Figure 3: F-structure for example (3)

2.4 Left-Right Context Rules

The left-right context annotation module is based on a tripartite division of local subtrees into a left-hand-side context (LHS) followed by a head (H) followed by a right-hand-side context (RHS). We developed our own head finding, or head lexicalization, rules based on a variety of heuristics and manual inspection of the PS rules.

Initially, we extracted 45785 Phrase Structure (PS) rules from the treebank. The reason for the relatively large number of PS rules is the fine-grained nature of the tags encoding morphological information for pre-terminal nodes. When we conflate pre-terminals containing morphological information to basic POS tags, the set of PS rules is reduced to 9731.
Treebanks grammars follow the Zipfian law: for each category, there is a small number of highly frequent rules expanding that category, followed by a large number of rules with a very low frequency. Therefore, for each LHS category we select the most frequent rules which together give 85% coverage. This results is a reduced set of 339 (most frequent) PS rules. These rules are manually examined and used to construct left-right LFG f-structure annotation matrices for the treebank. The annotation matrices encode information about

the left and right context of a rule's head and state generalisations about the functional annotation of constituents to the left and right of the local head.

Consider sentence (5), where an NP is expanded as NP NP ADJP. The first NP is considered the head and is given the annotation ↑=↓. The second NP and the ADJP are located to the left (Arabic reading) of the head (LHS). The left-right context matrix for NP constituents analyses these phrases as adjuncts and assigns them the annotation ↓ ∈ ↑ ADJUNCT.

(5) جمعيّة الطيّارين الأنغوليّة
jamoEiy~apu Al-Tay~Ariyna Al->anoguwliy~apu
society the-pilot the-Angolian
'Angolian Pilot Society'

The left-right annotation matrices also cover other non-subcategorisable functions (such as XADJUNCT, SPEC, etc.) as well as constituents with subcategorisable grammatical functions (SUBJ, OBJ, OBL, COMP, etc.) which are not identified via ATB functional tags (and hence left unannotated by the Functional Tags component)

2.5 Coordination

Treebanks tend to encode co-ordination in a rather flat manner. In the LFG framework coordinated constituents are treated as sets. The phrase structure functional annotations for creating a set function for such constituents is given in (6) where the f-structures of the two coordinated NPs on the right-hand side are members of the set valued f-structure of the NP on the left-hand side.

```
(6) NP → NP   CONJ NP
         ↑∈↓       ↑∈↓
```

To keep the other modules simple and perspicuous coordination is treated in the annotation algorithm as a separate component. The coordination module localizes the coordinating conjunct, marks it as head and adds the coordinated elements to the f-structure set representation of the coordination ↓∈↑ COORD. Figure 2.5 shows the f-structure for the NP in sentence (7).

(7)الكرات والتسديدات
Al-kurAtu wa-Al-tasodiydAtu
the-balls and-the-scores

```
[COORD_FORM  'wa-'                                          ]
[            { [PRED  'Al-kurAtu'     ]                    } ]
[            { [NUM   pl              ]                    } ]
[            { [GEND  fem             ]                    } ]
[            { [CASE  nom             ]                    } ]
[COORD       {                                             } ]
[            { [PRED  'Al-tasodiydAtu']                    } ]
[            { [NUM   pl              ]                    } ]
[            { [GEND  fem             ]                    } ]
[            { [CASE  nom             ]                    } ]
```

Figure 4: An Arabic coordination example

2.6 Catch-All and Clean-Up

The previous components of the annotation algorithm give concise statements of linguistic generalisations, but sometimes they overgeneralise. Such overgeneralisations are detected and corrected by the Catch-All and Clean-Up component of the algorithm.
For example, the mutiword expression إلّا أنّ 'illaA 'anna 'but' is annotated in the treebank as two subsequent subordinating conjunctions: (SUB_CONJ 'illaA) (SUB_CONJ 'anna). In the f-structure annotation this leads to a conflict as to which lexical item should occupy the value of the SUBORD_FORM feature. The Catch-All and Clean-Up component sidelines the problem by moving the second part of the MWE to an adjunct position.

Another example is provided by quantifiers. In Arabic, quantifiers have the same syntactic structure as the construct state (similar to the genitive construction in English as in *the boys' book*), so that sentences (8) and (9) are syntactically equivalent. The word 'students' is in the second part of the construct state in both phrases, but it is a modifier in the first and a head in the second. Therefore, a list of quantifiers (Table 3) is used in the Catch-All and Clean-Up module, so that they are identified and properly annotated according to certain context conditions.

The Catch-All and Clean-Up module also provides default annotations for nodes that remain unannotated by the previous components.
(8)كتب الطلّاب
kutubu Al-Tul~abi
books the-students
'students' books'

بعض الطلّاب (9)

baEoDu Al-Tul~abi

some the-students

'some students'

biDoEapu	بضعة	some
kAf~apu	كافّة	all
>ay~u	أيّ	any
jamiyEu	جميع	all
muEoZamu	معظم	most
biDoEu	بضع	few
kul~u	كلّ	all
baEoDu	بعض	some
baqiy~apu	بقيّة	rest
nafosu	نفس	same
>aHadu	أحد	one-masc
<iHodaY	إحدى	one-fem

Table 3: List of Arabic quantifiers

2.7 Traces

The f-structure generated prior to the Traces module is called a proto-f-structure (i.e. a partial representation), as it is not complete with respect to long-distance dependency resolution. In order to produce proper f-structures, long-distance dependencies such as topicalisation and wh-movement must be captured. In our annotation algorithm we exploit trace information in the ATB treebank and translate long-distance dependencies into cooresponding reentrancies at the f-structure level using coindexation.

Figure 5 gives the ATB tree for the phrase in (10) containing a trace. The trace is used to capture A-movement, and the indices on the WHNP-2 and NP-SBJ-2 indicate that these constituents are related.

In the annotation algorithm we assign the equation ↑SUBJ = ↑TOPICREL to the empty node to indicate that the relative pronoun 'which' is interpreted as the subject of the verb 'threaten'. This annotation produces the proper f-structure in Figure 6.

العنف الّذي يهدّد السلام (10)

Al-Eunofu Al~a*iy yuhad~idu Al-salAma

violence which threatens peace

Once every node in a tree is annotated with f-structure equations, the equations are then passed

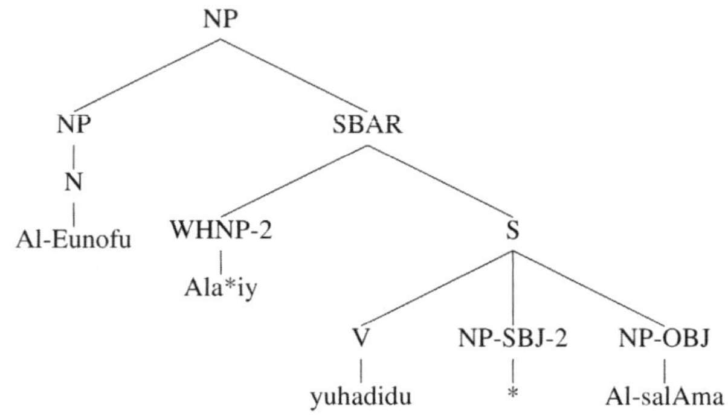

Figure 5: C-structure with a long-distance dependency

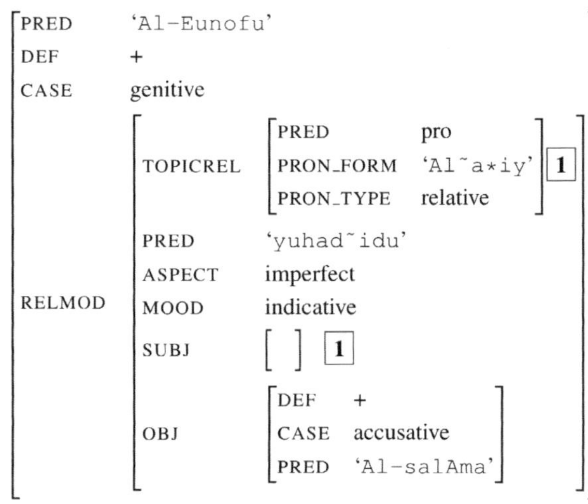

Figure 6: Proper f-structure with long-distance dependencies captured

to a constraint solver. Ideally one f-structure representation is produced for each sentence. If there are conflicts in the f-structure equations, no f-structure is produced.

3 Evaluation

We conduct two types of evaluation: quantitative and qualitative evaluation.

The quantitative evaluation evaluates the coverage of our annotation algorithm, while the qualitative evaluation compares the f-structures generated by the automatic annotation procedure against a gold standard of manually constructed f-structures for 250 sentences (Al-Raheb and al., 2006) selected at random from the ATB treebank. The aim of the qualitative evaluation is to ensure that the annotation quality is of a high standard, particularly as the annotation algorithm is used for extracting

wide-coverage syntactic and lexical resources.
In the quantitative evaluation experiment, the annotation algorithm achieves good coverage for 19 273 ATB sentences (remaining after removing trees with FRAG and X - labeled constituents); 98% of trees produce a complete and connected f-structure (no fragments) and 2% of trees do not produce an f-structure because of feature-value clashes.
For the qualitative evaluation, we use the evaluation methodology of (Crouch and al., 2002) and (Riezler, 2002) in order to calculate precision and recall on descriptions of f-structures. In this methodology, each f-structure is represented as a set of triples of the form: relation(argument$_1$,argument$_2$). For example the triples num(riHol+At+i, pl), case(riHol+At+i, genitive), gender(riHol+At+i, fem) encode that the number of the word riHol+At+i رحلات 'journeys' is plural; its case is genitive; and its gender is feminine. The triple subj(ta+bolug+u: *to reach*,HarAr+ap+a: *temperature*) indicates that the subject of the verb to reach is temperature. The results of the evaluation of the quality of the annotation against the DCU 250 gold standard are presented in Table 4. We achieve an f-score of 95%. In comparison, the f-scores for French, English and Chinese languages are 95%-96%. Table 5 presents the results by selected grammatical functions.

	Precision	**Recall**	**F-score**
Results	95.49	94.43	94.96

Table 4: Evaluation of the automatically produced f-structures against gold standard (all features).

	Precision	**Recall**	**F-score**
adjunct	91	91	91
coord	80	87	83
obj	81	88	85
obl	100	94	97
poss	96	89	92
subj	89	68	77
topic	93	92	92
topicrel	89	88	88

Table 5: Evaluation of the automatically produced f-structures against gold standard by selected grammatical functions.

4 Conclusion

In this paper, we have shown how the methodology for automatically annotating treebanks with LFG f-structure equations originally developed for English has been successfully adapted to Arabic. Arabic is known for its rich morphology and syntactic flexibility which allows SVO, VSO, VOS word orders. We exploit the rich morphological information in the annotation algorithm by utilising the morphological tags to add information to the f-structures. We also use ATB functional tags to specify default syntactic functions, e.g. -SBJ (subject) and -OBJ (object), provide left-right annotation matrices for the remaining constituents, treat coordination and represent non-local dependencies. The evaluation measured coverage as well as the quality of the automatic annotation algorithm. 98% of ATB trees (without FRAG and X) produce a complete and connected f-structure. When evaluated against a gold standard of 250 manually constructed f-structures, the algorithm scores an f-measure of 95%. The work presented in this paper is the first step in automatically acquiring deep resources for wide coverage parsing and generation for Arabic.

Acknowledgments

This research was supported by Science Foundation Ireland Grant 04/IN/I527.

References

Y. Al-Raheb, A. Akrout, J. van Genabith, J. Dichy. 2006. *DCU 250 Arabic Dependency Bank: An LFG Gold Standard Resource for the Arabic Penn Treebank* The Challenge of Arabic for NLP/MT at the British Computer Society, UK, pp. 105–116.

M. Attia. 2008. *Handling Arabic Morphological and Syntactic Ambiguity within the LFG Framework with a View to Machine Translation*. Ph.D. Thesis. The University of Manchester, Manchester, UK.

M. Baptista. 1995. *On the Nature of Pro-drop in Capeverdean Creole.* Harvard Working Papers in Linguistics, 5:3-17.

A. Bies and M. Maamouri. 2003. *Penn Arabic Treebank Guidelines* URL: http://www.ircs.upenn.edu/arabic/Jan03release/guidelines-TB-1-28-03.pdf.

J. Bresnan. 2001. *Lexical-Functional Syntax.* Blackwell Publishers, Oxford, UK.

M. Burke, O. Lam, R. Chan, A. Cahill, R. ODonovan, A. Bodomo, J. van Genabith, and A. Way. 2004. *Treebank-Based Acquisition of a Chinese Lexical-Functional Grammar.* The 18th Pacific Asia Conference on Language, Information and Computation, Tokyo, Japan, pp. 161–172.

M. Burke. 2006. *Automatic Treebank Annotation for the Acquisition of LFG Resources*. Ph.D. thesis, School of Computing, Dublin City University, Ireland.

A. Cahill, M. McCarthy, J. van Genabith, A. Way. 2002. *Automatic Annotation of the Penn Treebank with LFG F-Structure Information*. LREC Workshop on Linguistic Knowledge Acquisition and Representation: Bootstrapping Annotated Language Data, Spain, pp. 8-15.

A. Cahill, M. Forst, M. McCarthy, R. ODonovan, C. Rohrer, J. van Genabith and A. Way. 2003. *Treebank-Based Multilingual Unification Grammar Development*. The 15th Workshop on Ideas and Strategies for Multilingual Grammar Development, at the 15th European Summer School in Logic, Language and Information, Vienna, Austria, pp. 17–24.

A. Cahill, M. Burke, R. ODonovan, J. van Genabith, A. Way. 2004. *Long-Distance Dependency Resolution in Automatically Acquired Wide-Coverage PCFG-Based LFG Approximations*. 42nd Meeting of the Association for Computational Linguistics, Barcelona, Spain pp. 319-326.

A. Cahill, J. van Genabith. 2006. *Robust PCFG-Based Generation using Automatically Acquired LFG Approximations*. ACL 2006, Sydney, Australia, pages 1033-1040.

A. Cahill, M. Burke, R. O'Donovan, S. Riezler, J. van Genabith, A. Way. 2008. *Wide-Coverage Deep Statistical Parsing using Automatic Dependency Structure Annotation*. Computational Linguistics, Vol. 34, No. 1, pages 81-124.

N. Chomsky. 1981. *Lectures on Government and Binding*. Dordrecht: Foris.

G. Chrupala and J. van Genabith. 2006. *Improving Treebank-Based Automatic LFG Induction for Spanish*. In Proceedings of the LFG06 Conference.

R. Crouch, R. M. Kaplan, T. H. King, S. Riezler. 2002. *Comparison of Evaluation Metrics for a Broad Coverage Parser* LREC Workshop: Beyond PARSEVAL Towards Improved Evaluation Measures for Parsing Systems, Spain, pp. 67-74.

M. Dalrymple. 2002. *Lexical Functional Grammar*. Syntax and Semantics, Volume 34, Academic Press, San Diego, CA/London, U.K.

Y. Falk. 2001. *Lexical-Functional Grammar: An Introduction to Parallel Constraint-Based Syntax*. Stanford, Calif.: CSLI Publications.

A. Frank, L. Sadler, J. van Genabith, A. Way. 2003. *From Treebank Resources to LFG F-Structurese*. A. Abeille editor Treebanks: Building and Using Syntactically Annotated Corpora, Kluwer Academic Publishers, Dordrecht/Boston/London,The Netherlandsm pp. 367-389.

Y. Guo, J. van Genabith, H. Wang. 2007. *Acquisition of Wide-Coverage, Robust, Probabilistic Lexical-Functional Grammar Resources for Chinese*. Proceedings of the 12th International Lexical Functional Grammar Conference, USA, pp. 214–232.

R. Kaplan and J. Bresnan. 1982. *Lexical Functional Grammar: a Formal System for Grammatical Representation, in J. Bresnan (ed.)*. The Mental Representation of Grammatical Relations, MIT Press, Cambridge, MA, pp. 173-281.

R. M. Kaplan, S. Riezler, T. H. King, J. T. Maxwell, A. Vasserman, and R. Crouch. 2004. *Speed and Accuracy in Shallow and Deep Stochastic Parsing*. In The Human Language Technology Conference of the North American Chapter of the Association for Computational Linguistics (HLT-NAACL 2004), Boston, MA, pp. 97–104.

M. Maamouri and A. Bies. 2004. *Developing an Arabic Treebank: Methods, Guidelines, Procedures, and Tools* Workshop on Computational Approaches to Arabic Script-based Languages, COLING 2004, Geneva, 2004.

M. Marcus, G. Kim, M. Marcinkiewicz, R. MacIntyre, A. Bies, M. Ferguson, K. Katz and B. Schasberger 1994. *The Penn Treebank: Annotating Predicate Argument Structure*. In Proceedings of the Human Language Technology Workshop. San Francisco, CA.

R. O'Donovan, M. Burke, A. Cahill, J. van Genabith, and A. Way. 2004. *Large-Scale Induction and Evaluation of Lexical Resources from the Penn-II Treebank*. The 42nd Annual Meeting of the Association for Computational Linguistics, Barcelona, Spain, pp. 368–375.

R. O'Donovan, A. Cahill, J. van Genabith, and A. Way. 2005. *Automatic Acquisition of Spanish LFG Resources from the CAST3LB Treebank*. The Tenth International Conference on LFG, Bergen, Norway, pp. 334–352.

S. Riezler, King, T., Kaplan, R., Crouch, R., Maxwell, J. T., and Johnson, M. 2002. *Parsing theWall Street Journal using a Lexical-Functional Grammar and Discriminative Estimation Techniques*. The 40th Annual Conference of the Association for Computational Linguistics (ACL-02), Philadelphia, PA, pp. 271–278.

P. Sells 1985. *Lectures on Contemporary Syntactic Theories*. CSLI Lecture Notes. Stanford, CA: CSLI.

N. Schluter and J. van Genabith 2008. *Treebank-Based Acquisition of LFG Parsing Resources for French*. Proceedings of the Sixth International Language Resources and Evaluation (LREC'08).

Spoken Arabic Dialect Identification Using Phonotactic Modeling

Fadi Biadsy and **Julia Hirschberg**
Department of Computer Science
Columbia University, New York, USA
{fadi, julia}@cs.columbia.edu

Nizar Habash
Center for Computational Learning Systems
Columbia University, New York, USA
habash@ccls.columbia.edu

Abstract

The Arabic language is a collection of multiple variants, among which Modern Standard Arabic (MSA) has a special status as the formal written standard language of the media, culture and education across the Arab world. The other variants are informal spoken dialects that are the media of communication for daily life. Arabic dialects differ substantially from MSA and each other in terms of phonology, morphology, lexical choice and syntax. In this paper, we describe a system that automatically identifies the Arabic dialect (Gulf, Iraqi, Levantine, Egyptian and MSA) of a speaker given a sample of his/her speech. The phonotactic approach we use proves to be effective in identifying these dialects with considerable overall accuracy — 81.60% using 30s test utterances.

1 Introduction

For the past three decades, there has been a great deal of work on the automatic identification (ID) of languages from the speech signal alone. Recently, accent and dialect identification have begun to receive attention from the speech science and technology communities. The task of dialect identification is the recognition of a speaker's regional dialect, within a predetermined language, given a sample of his/her speech. The dialect-identification problem has been viewed as more challenging than that of language ID due to the greater similarity between dialects of the same language. Our goal in this paper is to analyze the effectiveness of a phonotactic approach, i.e. making use primarily of the rules that govern phonemes and their sequences in a language — a techniques which has often been employed by the language ID community — for the identification of Arabic dialects.

The Arabic language has multiple variants, including Modern Standard Arabic (MSA), the formal written standard language of the media, culture and education, and the informal spoken dialects that are the preferred method of communication in daily life. While there are commercially available Automatic Speech Recognition (ASR) systems for recognizing MSA with low error rates (typically trained on Broadcast News), these recognizers fail when a native Arabic speaker speaks in his/her regional dialect. Even in news broadcasts, speakers often *code switch* between MSA and dialect, especially in conversational speech, such as that found in interviews and talk shows. Being able to identify dialect vs. MSA as well as to identify which dialect is spoken during the recognition process will enable ASR engines to adapt their acoustic, pronunciation, morphological, and language models appropriately and thus improve recognition accuracy.

Identifying the regional dialect of a speaker will also provide important benefits for speech technology beyond improving speech recognition. It will allow us to infer the speaker's regional origin and ethnicity and to adapt features used in speaker identification to regional original. It should also prove useful in adapting the output of text-to-speech synthesis to produce regional speech as well as MSA – important for spoken dialogue systems' development.

In Section 2, we describe related work. In Section 3, we discuss some linguistic aspects of Arabic dialects which are important to dialect identification. In Section 4, we describe the Arabic dialect corpora employed in our experiments. In Section 5, we explain our approach to the identification of Arabic dialects. We present our experimental results in Section 6. Finally, we conclude in Section 7 and identify directions for future research.

2 Related Work

A variety of cues by which humans and machines distinguish one language from another have been explored in previous research on language identi-

Proceedings of the EACL 2009 Workshop on Computational Approaches to Semitic Languages, pages 53–61,
Athens, Greece, 31 March, 2009.

fication. Examples of such cues include phone inventory and phonotactics, prosody, lexicon, morphology, and syntax. Some of the most successful approaches to language ID have made use of phonotactic variation. For example, the Phone Recognition followed by Language Modeling (PRLM) approach uses phonotactic information to identify languages from the acoustic signal alone (Zissman, 1996). In this approach, a phone recognizer (not necessarily trained on a related language) is used to tokenize training data for each language to be classified. Phonotactic language models generated from this tokenized training speech are used during testing to compute language ID likelihoods for unknown utterances.

Similar cues have successfully been used for the identification of regional dialects. Zisssman et al. (1996) show that the PRLM approach yields good results classifying Cuban and Peruvian dialects of Spanish, using an English phone recognizer trained on TIMIT (Garofolo et al., 1993). The recognition accuracy of this system on these two dialects is 84%, using up to 3 minutes of test utterances. Torres-Carrasquillo et al. (2004) developed an alternate system that identifies these two Spanish dialects using Gaussian Mixture Models (GMM) with shifted-delta-cepstral features. This system performs less accurately (accuracy of 70%) than that of (Zissman et al., 1996). Alorfi (2008) uses an ergodic HMM to model phonetic differences between two Arabic dialects (Gulf and Egyptian Arabic) employing standard MFCC (Mel Frequency Cepstral Coefficients) and delta features. With the best parameter settings, this system achieves high accuracy of 96.67% on these two dialects. Ma et al. (2006) use multi-dimensional pitch flux features and MFCC features to distinguish three Chinese dialects. In this system the pitch flux features reduce the error rate by more than 30% when added to a GMM based MFCC system. Given 15s of test-utterances, the system achieves an accuracy of 90% on the three dialects.

Intonational cues have been shown to be good indicators to human subjects identifying regional dialects. Peters et al. (2002) show that human subjects rely on intonational cues to identify two German dialects (Hamburg urban dialects vs. Northern Standard German). Similarly, Barakat et al. (1999) show that subjects distinguish between Western vs. Eastern Arabic dialects significantly above chance based on intonation alone.

Hamdi et al. (2004) show that rhythmic differences exist between Western and Eastern Arabic. The analysis of these differences is done by comparing percentages of vocalic intervals (%V) and the standard deviation of intervocalic intervals (ΔC) across the two groups. These features have been shown to capture the complexity of the syllabic structure of a language/dialect in addition to the existence of vowel reduction. The complexity of syllabic structure of a language/dialect and the existence of vowel reduction in a language are good correlates with the rhythmic structure of the language/dialect, hence the importance of such a cue for language/dialect identification (Ramus, 2002).

As far as we could determine, there is no previous work that analyzes the effectiveness of a phonotactic approach, particularly the parallel PRLM, for identifying Arabic dialects. In this paper, we build a system based on this approach and evaluate its performance on five Arabic dialects (four regional dialects and MSA). In addition, we experiment with six phone recognizers trained on six languages as well as three MSA phone recognizers and analyze their contribution to this classification task. Moreover, we make use of a discriminative classifier that takes all the perplexities of the language models on the phone sequences and outputs the hypothesized dialect. This classifier turns out to be an important component, although it has not been a standard component in previous work.

3 Linguistic Aspects of Arabic Dialects

3.1 Arabic and its Dialects

MSA is the official language of the Arab world. It is the primary language of the media and culture. MSA is syntactically, morphologically and phonologically based on Classical Arabic, the language of the Qur'an (Islam's Holy Book). Lexically, however, it is much more modern. It is not a native language of any Arabs but is the language of education across the Arab world. MSA is primarily written not spoken.

The Arabic dialects, in contrast, are the true native language forms. They are generally restricted in use to informal daily communication. They are not taught in schools or even standardized, although there is a rich popular dialect culture of folktales, songs, movies, and TV shows. Dialects are primarily spoken, not written. However, this is changing as more Arabs gain access to electronic media such as emails and newsgroups. Arabic dialects are loosely related to Classical Arabic. They are the result of the interaction between different ancient dialects of Classical Arabic and other languages that existed in, neighbored and/or colonized what is today the Arab world. For example, Algerian Arabic has many influences from Berber as well as French.

Arabic dialects vary on many dimensions – primarily, geography and social class. Geolinguistically, the Arab world can be divided in many different ways. The following is only one of many that covers the main Arabic dialects:

- **Gulf Arabic** (GLF) includes the dialects of Kuwait, Saudi Arabia, Bahrain, Qatar, United Arab Emirates, and Oman.
- **Iraqi Arabic** (IRQ) is the dialect of Iraq. In some dialect classifications, Iraqi Arabic is considered a sub-dialect of Gulf Arabic.
- **Levantine Arabic** (LEV) includes the dialects of Lebanon, Syria, Jordan, Palestine and Israel.
- **Egyptian Arabic** (EGY) covers the dialects of the Nile valley: Egypt and Sudan.
- **Maghrebi Arabic** covers the dialects of Morocco, Algeria, Tunisia and Mauritania. Libya is sometimes included.

  Yemenite Arabic is often considered its own class. Maltese Arabic is not always considered an Arabic dialect. It is the only Arabic variant that is considered a separate language and is written with Latin script.

Socially, it is common to distinguish three subdialects within each dialect region: city dwellers, peasants/farmers and Bedouins. The three degrees are often associated with a class hierarchy from rich, settled city-dwellers down to Bedouins. Different social associations exist as is common in many other languages around the world.

The relationship between MSA and the dialect in a specific region is complex. Arabs do not think of these two as separate languages. This particular perception leads to a special kind of coexistence between the two forms of language that serve different purposes. This kind of situation is what linguists term *diglossia*. Although the two variants have clear domains of prevalence: formal written (MSA) versus informal spoken (dialect), there is a large gray area in between and it is often filled with a mixing of the two forms.

In this paper, we focus on classifying the dialect of audio recordings into one of five varieties: MSA, GLF, IRQ, LEV, and EGY. We do not address other dialects or diglossia.

3.2 Phonological Variations among Arabic Dialects

Although Arabic dialects and MSA vary on many different levels — phonology, orthography, morphology, lexical choice and syntax — we will focus on phonological difference in this paper.[1] MSA's phonological profile includes 28 consonants, three short vowels, three long vowels and two diphthongs (/ay/ and /aw/). Arabic dialects vary phonologically from standard Arabic and each other. Some of the common variations include the following (Holes, 2004; Habash, 2006):

The MSA consonant (/q/) is realized as a glottal stop /'/ in EGY and LEV and as /g/ in GLF and IRQ. For example, the MSA word /t̲ari:q/ 'road' appears as /t̲ari:'/ (EGY and LEV) and /t̲ari:g/ (GLF and IRQ). Other variants also are found in sub dialects such as /k/ in rural Palestinian (LEV) and /dj/ in some GLF dialects. These changes do not apply to modern and religious borrowings from MSA. For instance, the word for 'Qur'an' is never pronounced as anything but /qur'a:n/.

The MSA alveolar affricate (/dj/) is realized as /g/ in EGY, as /j/ in LEV and as /y/ in GLF. IRQ preserves the MSA pronunciation. For example, the word for 'handsome' is /djami:l/ (MSA, IRQ), /gami:l/ (EGY), /jami:l/ (LEV) and /yami:l/ (GLF).

The MSA consonant (/k/) is generally realized as /k/ in Arabic dialects with the exception of GLF, IRQ and the Palestinian rural sub-dialect of LEV, which allow a /č/ pronunciation in certain contexts. For example, the word for 'fish' is /samak/ in MSA, EGY and most of LEV but /simač/ in IRQ and GLF.

The MSA consonant /θ/ is pronounced as /t/ in LEV and EGY (or /s/ in more recent borrowings from MSA), e.g., the MSA word /θala:θa/ 'three' is pronounced /tala:ta/ in EGY and /tla:te/ in LEV. IRQ and GLF generally preserve the MSA pronunciation.

[1] It is important to point out that since Arabic dialects are not standardized, their orthography may not always be consistent. However, this is not a relevant point to this paper since we are interested in dialect identification using audio recordings and without using the dialectal transcripts at all.

The MSA consonant /δ/ is pronounced as /d/ in LEV and EGY (or /z/ in more recent borrowings from MSA), e.g., the word for 'this' is pronounced /ha:δa/ in MSA versus /ha:da/ (LEV) and /da/ EGY. IRQ and GLF generally preserve the MSA pronunciation.

The MSA consonants /d̲/ (emphatic/velarized d) and /δ̲/ (emphatic /δ/) are both normalized to /d̲/ in EGY and LEV and to /δ̲/ in GLF and IRQ. For example, the MSA sentence /δ̲alla yad̲rubu/ 'he continued to hit' is pronounced /d̲all yud̲rub/ (LEV) and /δ̲all yuδ̲rub/ (GLF). In modern borrowings from MSA, /δ̲/ is pronounced as /z̲/ (emphatic z) in EGY and LEV. For instance, the word for 'police officer' is /δ̲a:bit̲/ in MSA but /z̲a:bit̲/ in EGY and LEV.

In some dialects, a loss of the emphatic feature of some MSA consonants occurs, e.g., the MSA word /lat̲i:f/ 'pleasant' is pronounced as /lati:f/ in the Lebanese city sub-dialect of LEV. Emphasis typically spreads to neighboring vowels: if a vowel is preceded or succeeded directly by an emphatic consonant (/d̲/, /s̲/, /t̲/, /δ̲/) then the vowel becomes an emphatic vowel. As a result, the loss of the emphatic feature does not affect the consonants only, but also their neighboring vowels.

Other vocalic differences among MSA and the dialects include the following: First, short vowels change or are completely dropped, e.g., the MSA word /yaktubu/ 'he writes' is pronounced /yiktib/ (EGY and IRQ) or /yoktob/ (LEV). Second, final and unstressed long vowels are shortened, e.g., the word /mat̲a:ra:t/ 'airports' in MSA becomes /mat̲ara:t/ in many dialects. Third, the MSA diphthongs /aw/ and /ay/ have mostly become /o:/ and /e:/, respectively. These vocalic changes, particularly vowel drop lead to different syllabic structures. MSA syllables are primarily light (CV, CV:, CVC) but can also be (CV:C and CVCC) in utterance-final positions. EGY syllables are the same as MSA's although without the utterance-final restriction. LEV, IRQ and GLF allow heavier syllables including word initial clusters such as CCV:C and CCVCC.

4 Corpora

When training a system intended to classify languages or dialects, it is of course important to use training and testing corpora recorded under similar acoustic conditions. We are able to obtain corpora from the Linguistic Data Consortium (LDC) with similar recording conditions for four Arabic dialects: Gulf Arabic, Iraqi Arabic, Egyptian Arabic, and Levantine Arabic. These are corpora of spontaneous telephone conversations produced by native speakers of the dialects, speaking with family members, friends, and unrelated individuals, sometimes about predetermined topics. Although, the data have been annotated phonetically and/or orthographically by LDC, in this paper, we do not make use of any of annotations.

We use the speech files of 965 speakers (about 41.02 hours of speech) from the Gulf Arabic conversational telephone Speech database for our Gulf Arabic data (Appen Pty Ltd, 2006a).[2] From these speakers we hold out 150 speakers for testing (about 6.06 hours of speech).[3] We use the Iraqi Arabic Conversational Telephone Speech database (Appen Pty Ltd, 2006b) for the Iraqi dialect, selecting 475 Iraqi Arabic speakers with a total duration of about 25.73 hours of speech. From these speakers we hold out 150 speakers[4] for testing (about 7.33 hours of speech). Our Levantine data consists of 1258 speakers from the Arabic CTS Levantine Fisher Training Data Set 1-3 (Maamouri, 2006). This set contains about 78.79 hours of speech in total. We hold out 150 speakers for testing (about 10 hours of speech) from Set 1.[5] For our Egyptian data, we use CallHome Egyptian and its Supplement (Canavan et al., 1997) and CallFriend Egyptian (Canavan and Zipperlen, 1996). We use 398 speakers from these corpora (75.7 hours of speech), holding out 150 speakers for testing.[6] (about 28.7 hours of speech.)

Unfortunately, as far as we can determine, there is no data with similar recording conditions for MSA. Therefore, we obtain our MSA training data from TDT4 Arabic broadcast news. We use about 47.6 hours of speech. The acoustic signal was processed using forced-alignment with the transcript to remove non-speech data, such as music. For testing we again use 150 speakers, this time identified automatically from the GALE Year 2 Distillation evaluation corpus (about 12.06 hours of speech). Non-speech data (e.g., music) in the test

[2] We excluded very short speech files from the corpora.

[3] The 24 speakers in *devtest* folder and the last 63 files, after sorting by file name, in *train2c* folder (126 speakers). The sorting is done to make our experiments reproducible by other researchers.

[4] Similar to the Gulf corpus, the 24 speakers in *devtest* folder and the last 63 files (after sorting by filename) in *train2c* folder (126 speakers)

[5] We use the last 75 files in Set 1, after sorting by name.

[6] The test speakers were from *evaltest* and *devtest* folders in CallHome and CallFriend.

corpus was removed manually. It should be noted that the data includes read speech by anchors and reporters as well as spontaneous speech spoken in interviews in studios and though the phone.

5 Our Dialect ID Approach

Since, as described in Section 3, Arabic dialects differ in many respects, such as phonology, lexicon, and morphology, it is highly likely that they differ in terms of phone-sequence distribution and phonotactic constraints. Thus, we adopt the phonotactic approach to distinguishing among Arabic dialects.

5.1 PRLM for dialect ID

As mentioned in Section 2, the PRLM approach to language identification (Zissman, 1996) has had considerable success. Recall that, in the PRLM approach, the phones of the training utterances of a dialect are first identified using a single phone recognizer.[7] Then an n-gram language model is trained on the resulting phone sequences for this dialect. This process results in an n-gram language model for each dialect to model the dialect distribution of phone sequence occurrences. During recognition, given a test speech segment, we run the phone recognizer to obtain the phone sequence for this segment and then compute the perplexity of each dialect n-gram model on the sequence. The dialect with the n-gram model that minimizes the perplexity is hypothesized to be the dialect from which the segment comes.

Parallel PRLM is an extension to the PRLM approach, in which multiple (k) parallel phone recognizers, each trained on a different language, are used instead of a single phone recognizer (Zissman, 1996). For training, we run all phone recognizers in parallel on the set of training utterances of each dialect. An n-gram model on the outputs of each phone recognizer is trained for each dialect. Thus if we have m dialects, k x m n-gram models are trained. During testing, given a test utterance, we run all phone recognizers on this utterance and compute the perplexity of each n-gram model on the corresponding output phone sequence. Finally, the perplexities are fed to a combiner to determine the hypothesized dialect. In our implementation, we employ a logistic regression classifier as our back-end combiner. We have experimented with different classifiers such as SVM, and neural networks, but logistic regression classifier was superior. The system is illustrated in Figure 1.

We hypothesize that using multiple phone recognizers as opposed to only one allows the system to capture subtle phonetic differences that might be crucial to distinguish dialects. Particularly, since the phone recognizers are trained on different languages, they may be able to model different vocalic and consonantal systems, hence a different phonetic inventory. For example, an MSA phone recognizer typically does not model the phoneme /g/; however, an English phone recognizer does. As described in Section 3, this phoneme is an important cue to distinguishing Egyptian Arabic from other Arabic dialects. Moreover, phone recognizers are prone to many errors; relying upon multiple phone streams rather than one may lead to a more robust model overall.

5.2 Phone Recognizers

In our experiments, we have used phone recognizers for English, German, Japanese, Hindi, Mandarin, and Spanish, from a toolkit developed by Brno University of Technology.[8] These phone recognizers were trained on the OGI multilanguage database (Muthusamy et al., 1992) using a hybrid approach based on Neural Networks and Viterbi decoding without language models (open-loop) (Matejka et al., 2005).

Since Arabic dialect identification is our goal, we hypothesize that an Arabic phone recognizer would also be useful, particularly since other phone recognizers do not cover all Arabic consonants, such as pharyngeals and emphatic alveolars. Therefore, we have built our own MSA phone recognizer using the HMM toolkit (HTK) (Young et al., 2006). The monophone acoustic models are built using 3-state continuous HMMs without state-skipping, with a mixture of 12 Gaussians per state. We extract standard Mel Frequency Cepstral Coefficients (MFCC) features from 25 ms frames, with a frame shift of 10 ms. Each feature vector is 39D: 13 features (12 cepstral features plus energy), 13 deltas, and 13 double-deltas. The features are normalized using cepstral mean normalization. We use the Broadcast News TDT4 corpus (Arabic Set 1; 47.61 hours of speech; downsampled to 8Khz) to train our acoustic models. The

[7] The phone recognizer is typically trained on one of the languages being identified. Nonetheless, a phone recognize trained on any language might be a good approximation, since languages typically share many phones in their phonetic inventory.

[8] www.fit.vutbr.cz/research/groups/speech/sw/phnrec

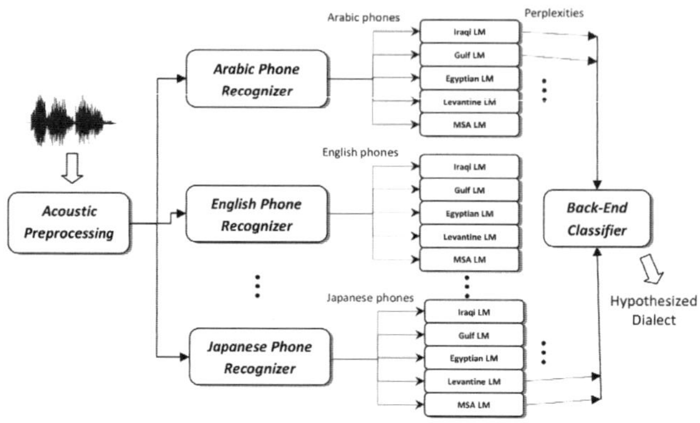

Figure 1: Parallel Phone Recognition Followed by Language Modeling (PRLM) for Arabic Dialect Identification.

pronunciation dictionary is generated as described in (Biadsy et al., 2009). Using these settings we build three MSA phone recognizers: (1) an open-loop phone recognizer which does not distinguish emphatic vowels from non-emphatic **(ArbO)**, (2) an open-loop with emphatic vowels **(ArbOE)**, and (3) a phone recognizer with emphatic vowels and with a bi-gram phone language model **(ArbLME)**. We add a new pronunciation rule to the set of rules described in (Biadsy et al., 2009) to distinguish emphatic vowels from non-emphatic ones (see Section 3) when generating our pronunciation dictionary for training the acoustic models for the the phone recognizers. In total we build 9 (Arabic and non-Arabic) phone recognizers.

6 Experiments and Results

In this section, we evaluate the effectiveness of the parallel PRLM approach on distinguishing Arabic dialects. We first run the nine phone recognizers described in Section 5 on the training data described in Section 4, for each dialect. This process produces nine sets of phone sequences for each dialect. In our implementation, we train a tri-gram language model on each phone set using the SRILM toolkit (Stolcke, 2002). Thus, in total, we have 9 x *(number of dialects)* tri-grams.

In all our experiments, the 150 test speakers of each dialect are first decoded using the phone recognizers. Then the perplexities of the corresponding tri-gram models on these sequences are computed, and are given to the logistic regression classifier. Instead of splitting our held-out data into test and training sets, we report our results with 10-fold cross validation.

We have conducted three experiments to evaluate our system. The first is to compare the performance of our system to Alorfi's (2008) on the same two dialects (Gulf and Egyptian Arabic). The second is to attempt to classify four colloquial Arabic dialects. In the third experiment, we include MSA as well in a five-way classification task.

6.1 Gulf vs. Egyptian Dialect ID

To our knowledge, Alorfi's (2008) work is the only work dealing with the automatic identification of Arabic dialects. In this work, an Ergodic HMM is used to model phonetic differences between Gulf and Egyptian Arabic using MFCC and delta features. The test and training data used in this work was collected from TV soap operas containing both the Egyptian and Gulf dialects and from twenty speakers from CallHome Egyptian database. The best accuracy reported by Alorfi (2008) on identifying the dialect of 40 utterances of duration of 30 seconds each of 40 male speakers (20 Egyptians and 20 Gulf speakers) is 96.67%.

Since we do not have access to the test collection used in (Alorfi, 2008), we test a version of our system which identifies these two dialects only on our 150 Gulf and 150 Egyptian speakers, as described in Section 4. Our best result is 97.00% (Egyptian and Gulf F-Measure = 0.97) when using only the features from the ArbOE, English, Japanese, and Mandarin phone recognizers. While our accuracy might not be *significantly* higher than that of Alorfi's, we note a few advantages of our experiments. First, the test sets of both dialects are from telephone conversations, with the same recording conditions, as opposed to a mix of different genres. Second, in our system we test 300 speakers as oppose to 40, so our results may be more reliable. Third, our test data includes female

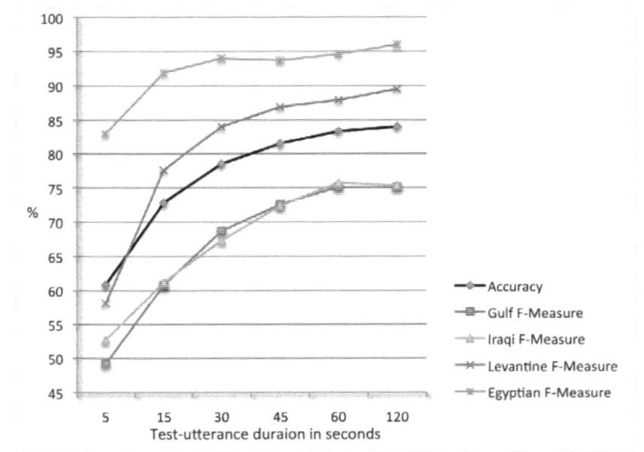

Figure 2: The accuracies and F-Measures of the four-way classification task with different test-utterance durations

speakers as well as male, so our results are more general.

6.2 Four Colloquial Arabic Dialect ID

In our second experiment, we test our system on four colloquial Arabic dialects (Gulf, Iraqi, Levantine, and Egyptian). As mentioned above, we use the phone recognizers to decode the training data to train the 9 tri-gram models per dialect (9x4=36 tri-gram models). We report our 10-fold cross validation results on the test data in Figure 2. To analyze how dependent our system is on the duration of the test utterance, we report the system accuracy and the F-measure of each class for different durations (5s – 2m). The longer the utterance, the better we expect the system to perform. We can observe from these results that regardless of the test-utterance duration, the best distinguished dialect among the four dialects is Egyptian (F-Measure of 94% with 30s test utterances), followed by Levantine (F-Measure of 84% with 30s), and the most confusable dialects, according to the classification confusion matrix, are those of the Gulf and Iraqi Arabic (F-Measure of 68.7%, 67.3%, respectively with 30s). This confusion is consistent with dialect classifications that consider Iraqi a sub-dialect of Gulf Arabic, as mentioned in Section 3.

We were also interested in testing which phone recognizers contribute the most to the classification task. We observe that employing a subset of the phone recognizers as opposed to all of them provides us with better results. Table 1 shows which phone recognizers are selected empirically, for each test-utterance duration condition.[9]

Dur.	Acc. (%)	Phone Recognizers
5s	60.83	ArbOE+ArbLME+G+H+M+S
15s	72.83	ArbOE+ArbLME+G+H+M
30s	78.50	ArbO+H+S
45s	81.5	ArbE+ArbLME+H+G+S
60s	83.33	ArbOE+ArbLME+E+G+H+M
120s	84.00	ArbOE+ArbLME+G+M

Table 1: Accuracy of the four-way classification (four colloquial Arabic dialects) and the best combination of phone recognizers used per test-utterances duration; The phone recognizers used are: E=English, G=German, H=Hindi, M=Mandarin, S=Spanish, ArbO=open-loop MSA without emphatic vowels, ArbOE=open-loop MSA with emphatic vowels, ArbLME=MSA with emphatic vowels and bi-gram phone LM

We observe that the MSA phone recognizers are the most important phone recognizers for this task, usually when emphatic vowels are modeled. In all scenarios, removing all MSA phone recognizers leads to a significant drop in accuracy. German, Mandarin, Hindi, and Spanish typically contribute to the classification task, but English, and Japanese phone recognizers are less helpful. It is possible that the more useful recognizers are able to capture more of the distinctions among the Arabic dialects; however, it might also be that the overall quality of the recognizers also varies.

6.3 Dialect ID with MSA

Considering MSA as a dialectal variant of Arabic, we are also interested in analyzing the performance of our system when including it in our classification task. In this experiment, we add MSA as the fifth dialect. We perform the same steps described above for training, using the MSA corpus described in Section 4. For testing, we use also our 150 hypothesized MSA speakers as our test set. Interestingly, in this five-way classification, we observe that the F-Measure for the MSA class in the cross-validation task is always above 98% regardless of the test-utterance duration, as shown in Figure 3.

It would seem that MSA is rarely confused with any of the colloquial dialects: it appears to have a distinct phonotactic distribution. This explanation is supported by linguists, who note that MSA differs from Arabic dialects in terms of its phonology, lexicon, syntax and morphology, which appears to lead to a profound impact on its phonotactic distribution. Similar to the four-way classification task,

[9] Starting from all phone recognizers, we remove one recognizer at a time; if the cross-validation accuracy decreases, we add it back. We have experimented with an automatic feature selection methods, but with the empirical ('greedy') selection we typically obtain higher accuracy.

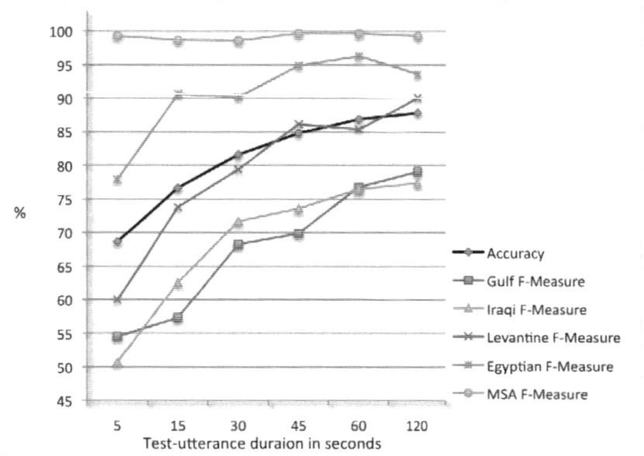

Figure 3: The accuracies and F-Measures of the five-way classification task with different test-utterance durations

Dur.	Acc. (%)	Phone Recognizers
5s	68.67	ArbO+ArbLME+H+M
15s	76.67	ArbLME+G+H+J+M
30s	81.60	ArbO+ArbOE+E+G+H+J+M+S
45s	84.80	ArbOE+ArbLME+E+G+H+J+M+S
60s	86.93	ArbOE+ArbLME+G+J+M+S
120s	87.86	ArbO+ArbLME+E+S

Table 2: Accuracy of the five-way classification (4 colloquial Arabic dialects + MSA) and the best combination of phone recognizers used per test-utterances duration; The phone recognizers used are: E=English, G=German, H=Hindi, J=Japanese, M=Mandarin, S=Spanish, ArbO=open-loop MSA without emphatic vowels, ArbOE=open-loop MSA with emphatic vowels, ArbLME=MSA with emphatic vowels and bi-gram phone LM

Egyptian was the most easily distinguished dialect (F-Measure=90.2%, with 30s test utterance) followed by Levantine (79.4%), and then Iraqi and Gulf (71.7% and 68.3%, respectively). Due to the high MSA F-Measure, the five-way classifier can also be used as a binary classifier to distinguish MSA from colloquial Arabic (Gulf, Iraqi, Levantine, and Egyption) reliably.

It should be noted that our classification results for MSA might be inflated for several reasons: (1) The MSA test data were collected from Broadcast News, which includes read (anchor and reporter) speech, as well as telephone speech (for interviews). (2) The identities of the test speakers in the MSA corpus were determined automatically, and so might not be as accurate.

As a result of the high identification rate of MSA, the overall accuracy in the five-way classification task is higher than that of the four-way classification. Table 2 presents the phone recognizers selected the accuracy for each test utterance duration. We observe here that the most important phone recognizers are those trained on MSA (ArbO, ArbOE, and/or ArbLME). Removing them completely leads to a significant drop in accuracy. In this classification task, we observe that all phone recognizers play a role in the classification task in some of the conditions.

7 Conclusions and Future Work

In this paper, we have shown that four Arabic colloquial dialects (Gulf, Iraqi, Levantine, and Egyptian) plus MSA can be distinguished using a phonotactic approach with good accuracy. The parallel PRLM approach we employ thus appears to be effective not only for language identification but also for Arabic dialect ID.

We have found that the most distinguishable dialect among the five variants we consider here is MSA, independent of the duration of the test-utterance (F-Measure is always above 98.00%). Egyptian Arabic is second (F-Measure of 90.2% with 30s test-utterances), followed by Levantine (F-Measure of 79.4%, with 30s test). The most confusable dialects are Iraqi and Gulf (F-Measure of 71.7% and 68.3%, respectively, with 30s test-utterances). This high degree of Iraqi-Gulf confusion is consistent with some classifications of Iraqi Arabic as a sub-dialect of Gulf Arabic. We have obtained a total accuracy of 81.60% in this five-way classification task when given 30s-duration utterances. We have also observed that the most useful phone streams for classification are those of our Arabic phone recognizers — typically those with emphatic vowels.

As mentioned above, the high F-measure for MSA may be due to the MSA corpora we have used, which differs in genre from the dialect corpora. Therefore, one focus of our future research will be to collect MSA data with similar recording conditions to the other dialects to validate our results. We are also interested in including prosodic features, such as intonational, durational, and rhythmic features in our classification. A more long-term and general goal is to use our results to improve ASR for cases in which code-switching occurs between MSA and other dialects.

Acknowledgments

We thank Dan Ellis, Michael Mandel, and Andrew Rosenberg for useful discussions. This material is based upon work supported by the Defense Advanced Research Projects Agency (DARPA) under Contract No. HR0011-06-C-0023 (approved for public release, distribution unlimited). Any opinions, findings and conclusions or recommendations expressed in this material are those of the authors and do not necessarily reflect the views of DARPA.

References

F. S. Alorfi. 2008. PhD Dissertation: Automatic Identification Of Arabic Dialects Using Hidden Markov Models. In *University of Pittsburgh*.

Appen Pty Ltd. 2006a. Gulf Arabic Conversational Telephone Speech Linguistic Data Consortium, Philadelphia.

Appen Pty Ltd. 2006b. Iraqi Arabic Conversational Telephone Speech Linguistic Data Consortium, Philadelphia.

M. Barkat, J. Ohala, and F. Pellegrino. 1999. Prosody as a Distinctive Feature for the Discrimination of Arabic Dialects. In *Proceedings of Eurospeech'99*.

F. Biadsy, N. Habash, and J. Hirschberg. 2009. Improving the Arabic Pronunciation Dictionary for Phone and Word Recognition with Linguistically-Based Pronunciation Rules. In *Proceedings of NAACL/HLT 2009, Colorado, USA*.

A. Canavan and G. Zipperlen. 1996. CALLFRIEND Egyptian Arabic Speech Linguistic Data Consortium, Philadelphia.

A. Canavan, G. Zipperlen, and D. Graff. 1997. CALLHOME Egyptian Arabic Speech Linguistic Data Consortium, Philadelphia.

J. S. Garofolo et al. 1993. TIMIT Acoustic-Phonetic Continuous Speech Corpus Linguistic Data Consortium, Philadelphia.

N. Habash. 2006. On Arabic and its Dialects. *Multilingual Magazine*, 17(81).

R. Hamdi, M. Barkat-Defradas, E. Ferragne, and F. Pellegrino. 2004. Speech Timing and Rhythmic Structure in Arabic Dialects: A Comparison of Two Approaches. In *Proceedings of Interspeech'04*.

C. Holes. 2004. *Modern Arabic: Structures, Functions, and Varieties*. Georgetown University Press. Revised Edition.

B. Ma, D. Zhu, and R. Tong. 2006. Chinese Dialect Identification Using Tone Features Based On Pitch Flux. In *Proceedings of ICASP'06*.

M. Maamouri. 2006. Levantine Arabic QT Training Data Set 5, Speech Linguistic Data Consortium, Philadelphia.

P. Matejka, P. Schwarz, J. Cernocky, and P. Chytil. 2005. Phonotactic Language Identification using High Quality Phoneme Recognition. In *Proceedings of Eurospeech'05*.

Y. K. Muthusamy, R.A. Cole, and B.T. Oshika. 1992. The OGI Multi-Language Telephone Speech Corpus. In *Proceedings of ICSLP'92*.

J. Peters, P. Gilles, P. Auer, and M. Selting. 2002. Identification of Regional Varieties by Intonational Cues. An Experimental Study on Hamburg and Berlin German. 45(2):115–139.

F. Ramus. 2002. Acoustic Correlates of Linguistic Rhythm: Perspectives. In *Speech Prosody*.

A. Stolcke. 2002. SRILM - an Extensible Language Modeling Toolkit. In *ICASP'02*, pages 901–904.

P. Torres-Carrasquillo, T. P. Gleason, and D. A. Reynolds. 2004. Dialect identification using Gaussian Mixture Models. In *Proceedings of the Speaker and Language Recognition Workshop, Spain*.

S. Young, G. Evermann, M. Gales, D. Kershaw, G. Moore, J. Odell, D. Ollason, D. Povey, V. Valtchev, and P. Woodland. 2006. The HTK Book, version 3.4.

M. A. Zissman, T. Gleason, D. Rekart, and B. Losiewicz. 1996. Automatic Dialect Identification of Extemporaneous Conversational, Latin American Spanish Speech. In *Proceedings of the IEEE International Conference on Acoustics, Speech, and Signal Processing*, Atlanta, USA.

M. A. Zissman. 1996. Comparison of Four Approaches to Automatic Language Identification of Telephone Speech. *IEEE Transactions of Speech and Audio Processing*, 4(1).

Structure-based evaluation of an Arabic semantic Query Expansion using the JIRS Passage Retrieval system

Lahsen ABOUENOUR
Mohammadia School of Engineers, Med Vth University
Rabat, Morocco
abouenour@yahoo.fr

Karim Bouzoubaa
Mohammadia School of Engineers, Med Vth University
Rabat, Morocco
karim.bouzoubaa@emi.ac.ma

Paolo Rosso
Natural Language Engineering Lab, ELiRF, Universidad Politécnica
Valencia, Spain
prosso@dsic.upv.es

Abstract

The adoption of semantic Query Expansion (QE) could be useful in the context of Question/Answering (Q/A) systems. For the Arabic language this is a challenging task since it has many particularities (short vowels, absence of capital letters, complex morphology, etc.). This paper presents an evaluation of a proposed semantic QE based on Arabic WordNet (AWN). Two types of experiments are conducted: the keyword-based evaluation which uses a classical search engine as passage retrieval system, and the structure-based evaluation that uses the Java Information Retrieval System (JIRS) which takes into account the structure of the question. Results show that the best performances in terms of accuracy and Mean Reciprocal Rank are reached when the proposed semantic QE together with JIRS are used.

1 Introduction

With the fast growing of the available content on the web, there is an increasing interest in Question/Answering systems (Q/A) (Carbonell et al., 2000). In fact, classical Information Retrieval (IR) systems are wasteful when users look for a precise answer of a question instead of a set of returned documents.

Unlike other languages such as English, the research in Arabic Natural Language Processing (NLP) has, so far, concentrated less on the Q/A task. Nevertheless, there are a number of attempts to implement automatic Arabic Q/A systems working on structured texts (Mohammed et al., 1993), returning relevant snippets without automatically extracting answers (Hammou et al., 2002), (Benajiba et al., 2007a) as well as recently a semi-automatic Q/A system for factoid questions (Brini et al., to appear in 2009). Most of these systems are based on three modules: question classification and analysis, passage retrieval (PR) and answer extraction. The performance of the latter depends on the results provided by the two first modules. Indeed, if the retrieved passages returned by the second module do not contain the whole or a part of the question keywords, the answer extraction module fails to provide the expected answer.

Most of the time, users concretely formulate the question using words which do not, necessarily, appear in the base documents. Therefore, a Query Expansion (QE) process could be used by the Q/A system modules in order to generate new keywords that may exist in the base documents. Rachidi et al. (2003) cite statistical and dictionary-based QE techniques as the most common for Arabic. These techniques could be useful in the context of Q/A systems. Unfortunately, keywords which are semantically related to the user question may not be provided by a basic QE. Indeed, even if those keywords could be relevant, a QE which uses only lexical and morphological resources might not be able to identify them. Thus, the use of a semantic QE is required since the same question can be formulated using different words with an equivalent meaning. Moreover, the generation of keywords based on the semantic relations makes easier the matching of the question structure and the candidate passages one.

In (Abouenour et al., 2008) we have presented a semantic QE approach with preliminary experiments in the context of the Arabic Q/A task. This approach uses the current release of the Arabic

Proceedings of the EACL 2009 Workshop on Computational Approaches to Semitic Languages, pages 62–68,
Athens, Greece, 31 March, 2009.

WordNet[1] ontology (AWN) (Elkateb et al., 2006; Rodriguez et al., 2008). Let us recall briefly that AWN ontology is a free lexical resource for modern standard Arabic (Elkateb et al., 2006). It is based on the design and contents of Princeton WordNet (PWN) (Fellbaum, 2000) and can be mapped onto PWN as well as a number of other wordnets, enabling translation on the lexical level to and from dozens of other languages. AWN is also connected to SUMO (Supper Upper Merged Ontology) (Niles and Pease, 2001; Niles and Pease, 2003).

Our approach uses not only the current content of AWN but also four of its semantic relations. Indeed, we use a QE process based on: (i) QE by synonyms, (ii) QE by definitions, (iii) QE by subtypes, (iv) QE by supertypes.

In order to be able, in further works, to consider other semantic operations, we have implemented our approach using the Amine Platform[2]. Amine is a Java open source multi-layer platform dedicated to the development of intelligent systems and multi-agents systems (Kabbaj et al., 2006). Thus, the Amine AWN (AAWN) hierarchy is based on the content and the structure of AWN. For each concept type in AAWN there are synonyms, subtypes and supertypes with respect to the synonymy, hyponymy and hypernymy relations in AWN. The implementation of QE by definition uses the SUMO concepts definitions written in SUO-KIF notation.

The added value of this semantic QE in the context of Arabic Q/A systems has been illustrated by examples in (Abouenour et al., 2008). We have conducted preliminary experiments with 82 CLEF[3] questions with manual search using Google Search Engine (SE).

In the community and in order to evaluate the results, two measures are considered:

- The Accuracy which is the average of the questions where we find the right answer in the first snippet;
- The Mean Reciprocal Rank (MRR). The reciprocal rank of a query response is the multiplicative inverse of the rank of the correct answer: MRR is the average of the reciprocal ranks of results for a sample of queries[4] (Voorhees, 1999).

The results have shown that the semantic QE based on AAWN ontology has improved the accuracy by 3,66 % and the MRR by 1,10. Preliminary experiments consider keywords separately without taking into account the question structure. The Java Information Retrieval System (JIRS[5]) (Benajiba et al., 2007b) is a passage retrieval system which can allow us to consider this structure.

Our general aim is to develop a separate semantic QE module that could be used within Q/A systems. In the context of the current paper, our objective is two fold: (i) confirm previous results with large and automatic experiments using the Yahoo API; (ii) take into account the structure of the question and retrieved passages using JIRS.

The structure of this paper is as follows: in Section 2 we give more details about the evaluation and the refinement process of our semantic Query Expansion. Section 3 is devoted to the results of the automatic evaluation based only on keywords. In Section 4, we present the results of the structure-based evaluation. Section 5 is a synthesis of the results reached in the two experiments. Finally, in the last section we draw some conclusions and we discuss the future works to be done.

2 Evaluation and refinement process of our semantic Query Expansion

The tasks related to the design of our semantic Query Expansion are illustrated in Figure 1.

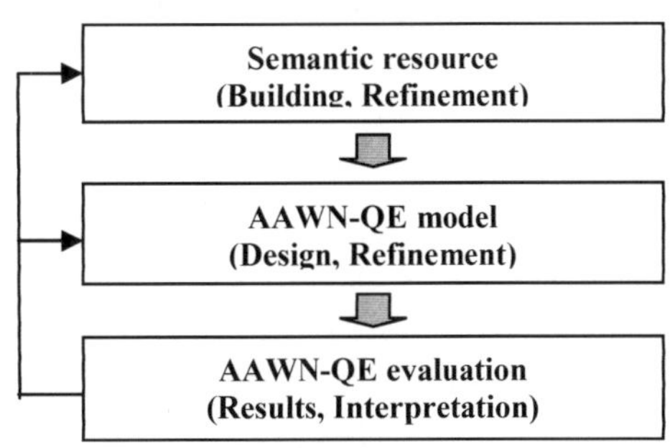

Figure 1. The proposed semantic QE approach

The above figure shows that one of the evaluation process aims is evaluating both the QE

[1] http://www.globalwordnet.org/AWN/
[2] http://amine-platform.sourceforge.net
[3] Cross Language Evaluation Forum, http://www.clef-campaign.org
[4] http://en.wikipedia.org/wiki/Mean_reciprocal_rank
[5] http://sourceforge.net/projects/jirs/

model and the semantic resource used. With respect to the semantic resource level, the current release of AWN (Elkateb et al., 2006) allows to work with around 20,000 words grouped into 10,000 synsets.

At the experiments level, the current evaluation process uses a set of 82 CLEF questions that was translated into Arabic[6]. These CLEF questions are classified into different domains (sport, geography, politic, etc.) and different types (questions seeking for time answers, persons, places, etc.) as illustrated in Table 1. The considered questions are related to different topics and, therefore, present a significant coverage.

Domains	# Q	%
History	20	24,69
Sport	5	6,17
Politic	12	14,81
Culture	9	11,11
Geography	8	9,88
Technology	7	8,64
Other	21	25,93

Table 1. The distribution of the considered question per domain

Actually, we did not use any specific Q/A system. However, in order to simulate the use of our QE module within Q/A systems, we carried out the following experiment process: we manually select the most relevant keywords of each question. The given keywords are, then, extended using our semantic Query Expansion process. After that, the answer of each question and extended question is searched within the first five snippets returned by the used Passage Retrieval (PR) system. In the keyword-based evaluation process only a search engine (Yahoo[7]) is used as PR system (the returned snippets are considered in the evaluation).

In the structure-based evaluation process, JIRS is used. Indeed, JIRS is a language-independent PR system which has been already adapted to a few non-agglutinative European languages (such as English and French) as well as to the Arabic language (Benajiba et al., 2007b). The re-ranking of the retrieved passages is based on a distance density n-gram model. In (Benajiba et al., 2007b) authors explain the idea of this model which gives more weight to the passages where the most relevant question structures appear nearer to each other. In (Gomez et al., 2007) some experiments were carried out to re-rank snippets obtained with Yahoo in order to return the most relevant ones containing the answer.

In the next section we present the results obtained with an automatic evaluation process using the Yahoo search engine.

3 Keyword-based experiments

In this section, we investigate whether or not the semantic Query Expansion succeeded in improving results with respect to when no semantic QE is employed.

Type QE	Accuracy	MRR
Without Semantic QE	**1,22%**	**0,99**
QE by Synonyms	3,66%	1,63
QE by Definitions	4,88%	2,16
QE by Subtypes	4,88%	2,39
QE by Supertypes	8,54%	3,49
Overall Semantic QE	**7,32%**	**3,25**

Table 2. Experiment results of AAWN Query Expansion using Yahoo API

Table 2 shows the results of the experiments using the Yahoo API. The poor performance obtained is due to the fact that some relaxations are not used when we perform an automatic process. For example, in the manual process we can identify answers composed of more than one word. For example, the answer of the question "كم تبلغ القيمة المادية لجائزة المغرب للكتاب" (What is the value of the Moroccan book award?) is "7000 دولار". If a snippet contains for instance the expression "سبعة ألاف دولار" the answer is considered correct.

Nevertheless, even with an automatic process, the use of AAWN Query Expansion has improved the accuracy (from 1,22% to 7,32%) and the MRR (from 0,99 to 3,25). Moreover, the use of only one type of semantic QE already improves of the considered measures. For instance, the QE by synonym reaches an accuracy of 3,66 % (against 1,22% without QE) and 1,63 as MRR (against 0,99 without QE).
We can also notice that among the four semantic types of QE the one by supertypes gives the best results in term of accuracy and MRR as well. The ranking of the four semantic types of QE is the same with respect to the accuracy measure or the MRR.

[6] http://www.dsic.upv.es/grupos/nle/downloads.html
[7] www.yahoo.com

Table 3 shows the statistics related to the average of the number of generated keywords per question and per type of QE. It lists also the number of answered question per type of QE.

Type QE	Avg (keywords/Q)	#Answered Questions
By Synonyms	2,28	10
By Definitions	0,99	14
By subtypes	1,05	16
By supertypes	1,24	18
Semantic QE	5,56	18
Without QE	0	8

Table 3. Answered questions per type of QE using Yahoo API

For 21,95% of the considered questions the answer was found (in one of the first five snippets) after using the semantic QE. Without semantic QE we reach only a percentage of 9,76 %.

In Figure 2 we present graphically statistics related to the average of the number of generated keywords per question and per type of QE. Although the QE by synonyms generates an average of 2,28 keywords per question, the number of answered question using this semantic relation is the least among the four relations. Their ranking with respect to the number of answered question is the same as the accuracy and MRR measures.

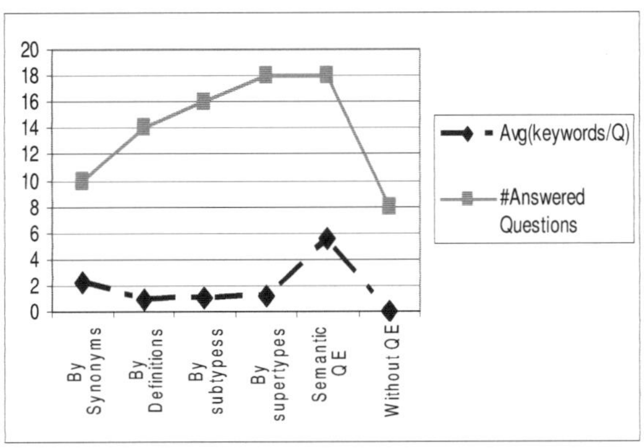

Figure 2. Answered questions per type of QE using the Yahoo API

In the next section we perform the same experiments using the JIRS PR system which considers the comparison of the returned passages structure with the one of the question.

4 Structure-based experiments

In the previous section we have considered only the first five snippets. However, the expected answer could exist in the returned results but not in these first five snippets. As we already mentioned, Gomez et al. (2007) have carried out preliminary experiments that show how JIRS PR system helps to re-rank Yahoo search engine snippets in order to make easier the answer extraction. Indeed, they have showed that the distance density n-gram model of JIRS improves both the coverage and the redundancy of the answers.

In these experiments, we have built a corpus based on the first 1,000 returned snippets by Yahoo. For the 82 CLEF questions, we have obtained an average of 42.96 returned snippets per question. After applying the JIRS indexation process to the built corpus, we have carried out the same experiments of the previous section, but using the JIRS PR system instead of the Yahoo API. Table 4 below shows the new results reached.

Type QE	Accuracy	MRR
Without Semantic QE	**15,85%**	**5,46**
QE by Synonyms	18,29%	6,72
QE by Definitions	9,76%	3,54
QE by Subtypes	8,54%	3,93
QE by Supertypes	13,41%	5,35
Overall Semantic QE	**19,51%**	**7,85**

Table 4: Experiment results of AAWN Query Expansion using the JIRS

Comparing the new results with the previous ones, the accuracy and the MRR have been improved even when we did not use any QE. The use of the proposed semantic QE together with JIRS improves the relevance of the first five snippets returned by the search engine. Therefore, the snippets are re-ranked better.

The results show that the proposed semantic Query Expansion continues to improve the accuracy and the MRR even if with different types of PR. The whole semantic QE has obtained an accuracy of 19,51% (against 15,85% without QE) and an MRR of 7,85 (against 5,46 without QE).

On the other hand, the QE by synonyms has provided the best results unlike the previous experiments. Indeed, the obtained accuracy is 18,29% and the MRR is 6,72. The ranking of the

QE types has changed, and the supertype-based QE provides, in this case, the second best performance instead of the first one.

In Table 5 and Figure 3 we show the statistics regarding the number of answered questions.

Type QE	Avg (keywords /Q)	#Answered Questions
QE by Synonym	2,28	22
QE by Definition	0,99	12
QE by subtypes	1,05	14
QE by supertypes	1,24	19
Overall Semantic QE	5,56	24
Without QE	0	23

Table 5. Answered question per type of QE using JIRS

The number of answered questions has passed to 24 (against 18 previously) in the case of semantic QE. However, the number of answered questions in the case of not using QE is approximately the same.

The ranking of the semantic QE types according to this measure confirms the one obtained with the accuracy and the MRR.

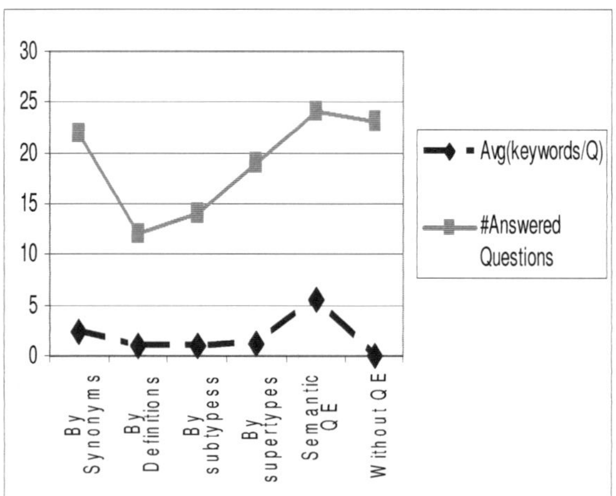

Figure 3. Answered questions per type of QE using the JIRS

Figure 3 shows that the number of answered questions does not clearly depend on the number of used keywords.

5 Synthesis of the evaluation results

In order to make a summarized comparison between the keyword-based experiment and the structure-based experiments, we have drawn the following tables (see table 6 and table 7):

Accuracy	Without JIRS	Using JIRS
Without Semantic QE	**1,22%**	15,85%
With Semantic QE	7,32%	**19,51%**

Table 6. Comparison of the Accuracy reached in the two experiments

MRR	Without JIRS	Using JIRS
Without Semantic QE	**0,99**	5,46
With Semantic QE	3,25	**7,85**

Table 7. Comparison of the MRR reached in the two experiments

Table 6 illustrates that the best accuracy and MRR (19,51% and 7,85) have been obtained when the semantic Query Expansion and the JIRS PR system are used together.

The results show that the stage of QE by synonyms was one of the two most successful semantic expansions with respect to the improvement of both the accuracy and the MRR. Moreover, there are some questions for which the answer does not appear in the first five snippets returned without using semantic QE.

6 Conclusion and Future Works

This work has been done in order to evaluate our proposed semantic QE for Arabic Q/A systems. Our aim was to confirm the preliminary experiments which showed that the accuracy and the MRR have been improved and that our semantic QE process (based on the current release of AWN) is adequate to improve the passage retrieval stage of an Arabic Q/A system.

This work has confirmed that, once more, the semantic QE improves both the accuracy and the MRR. In addition, in the case where it is combined with JIRS, our approach has obtained an accuracy around 19,51% and 7,85 as MRR. This means that when we take into account the semantic and the structure of the question we improve the probability of obtaining relevant passages (i.e., containing the answer).
The use of Arabic WordNet within the Amine Platform traces new ways regarding the semantic QE. As future work, we could take advantage of the concept definitions. Indeed, we could calcu-

late the similarity between the question and the returned passages according to a semantic comparison.

The proposed semantic QE approach does not define, so far, any weight to be assigned to the generated keywords. In the next steps of this work, we could decide on the relevance of each keyword according to its source (e.g. QE by supertypes could have the higher value) and the distance between the generated keyword and the initial one.

Finally, at the moment, the AWN project does not cover totally the standard Arabic. Therefore, the consideration of a completed version of AWN (Rodriguez et al., 2008) is to be intended.

Acknowledgement

This research was made possible thanks also to the following projects: AECI-PCI A010317/07, AECID PCI B017961/08 and CICYT TIN2006-15265-C06. We would like also to thank Dr. Manuel Gómez (Universidad Alicante, Spain) to help us with the use of JIRS.

References

Abouenour L., Bouzoubaa K., Rosso P. 2008. Improving Q/A Using Arabic Wordnet. In: Proc. *The 2008 International Arab Conference on Information Technology (ACIT'2008),* Tunisia, December.

Benajiba Y., Rosso P., Lyhyaoui A. 2007a. "Implementation of the ArabiQA Question Answering System's components", *In: Proc. Workshop on Arabic Natural Language Processing, 2nd Information Communication Technologies Int. Symposium, ICTIS-2007*, Fez, Morroco, April 3-5.

Benajiba Y., Rosso P., Gómez J.M. 2007b. "Adapting JIRS Passage Retrieval System to the Arabic". *In: Proc. 8th Int. Conf. on Comput. Linguistics and Intelligent Text Processing, CICLing-2007*, Springer-Verlag, LNCS(4394), pp. 530-541.

Brini W., Ellouze M., Hadrich Belguith L. 2009. *QA-SAL :* "Un système de question-réponse dédié pour les questions factuelles en langue Arabe*". In: 9ème Journées Scientifiques desJeunes Chercheurs en Génie Electrique et Informatique, Tunisia.* (To appear in March; in French).

Carbonell J., Harman D., Hovy E., Maiorano S., Prange J., Sparck-Jones K. 2000. "Vision Statement to Guide Research in Question & Answering (Q&A) and Text Summarization". Rapport technique, NIST.

Elkateb, S., Black W., Vossen P., Farwell D., Rodríguez H., Pease A., Alkhalifa M. 2006. "Arabic WordNet and the Challenges of Arabic". *In proceedings of Arabic NLP/MT Conference*, London, U.K.

Fellbaum C. 2000. "WordNet: An Electronic Lexical Database". *MIT Press, cogsci.princeton.edu/˜wn,* September 7.

Gómez J. M., Rosso P., Sanchis E. 2007. Re-ranking of Yahoo snippets with the JIRS Passage Retrieval system. In: Proc. Workshop on Cross Lingual Information Access, CLIA-2007, 20th Int. Joint Conf. on Artificial Intelligence, IJCAI-07, Hyderabad, India, January 6-12.

Hammou B., Abu-salem H., Lytinen S., Evens M. 2002. "QARAB: A Question answering system to support the ARABic language". *In: Proc. of the workshop on Computational approaches to Semitic languages, ACL*, pages 55-65, Philadelphia.

Kabbaj A., Bouzoubaa K., K. ElHachimi and N. Ourdani. 2006. "Ontology in Amine Platform: Structures and Processes", *In the 14th Proc. Int. Conf. Conceptual Structures, ICCS 2006*, Aalborg, Denmark.

Mohammed F.A., Nasser K., Harb H.M. 1993. "A knowledge-based Arabic Question Answering System (AQAS)". *In: ACM SIGART Bulletin*, pp. 21-33.

Niles I., Pease A. 2001. "Towards a Standard Upper Ontology". *In: Proceedings of FOIS 2001*, Ogunquit, Maine, pp. 2-9.

Niles I., Pease A. 2003. "Linking Lexicons and Ontologies: Mapping WordNet to the Suggested Upper Merged Ontology." *In Proceedings of the 2003 International Conference on Information and Knowledge Engineering*, Las Vegas, Nevada.

Rachidi T., M. Bouzoubaa, L. ElMortaji, B. Boussouab, and A. Bensaid. 2003. "Arabic user search Query correction and expansion", in Proc. of COPSTIC'03, Rabat December 11-13.

Rodríguez H., Farwell D., Farreres J., Bertran M., Alkhalifa M., Antonia Martí M., Black W., Elkateb S., Kirk J., Pease A., Vossen P., and Fell-

baum C. 2008. Arabic WordNet: Current State and Future Extensions in: Proceedings of the Fourth International GlobalWordNet Conference - GWC 2008, Szeged, Hungary, January 22-25, 2008.
http://www.lsi.upc.edu/~nlp/papers/rodriguez08a.pdf.

Rosso P., Benajiba Y., Lyhyaoui A. 2006 "Towards an Arabic Question Answering system (in Arabic)". *In: Proc. 4th Conf. on Scientific Research Outlook & Technology Development in the Arab world, SROIV*, Damascus, Syria, 11-14 December.

Voorhees E.M., "The TREC-8 question answering track report". 1999. *In Proceedings of the 8th Text Retrieval Conference*, Gaithersburg, Maryland, USA, pp. 77-82.

Syntactic Reordering for English-Arabic Phrase-Based Machine Translation

Jakob Elming
Languagelens
Copenhagen, Denmark
je@languagelens.com

Nizar Habash
Center for Computational Learning Systems
Columbia University, New York, USA
habash@ccls.columbia.edu

Abstract

We investigate syntactic reordering within an English to Arabic translation task. We extend a pre-translation syntactic reordering approach developed on a close language pair (English-Danish) to the distant language pair, English-Arabic. We achieve significant improvements in translation quality over related approaches, measured by manual as well as automatic evaluations. These results prove the viability of this approach for distant languages.

1 Introduction

The emergence of phrase-based statistical machine translation (PSMT) (Koehn et al., 2003a) has been one of the major developments in statistical approaches to translation. Allowing translation of word sequences (phrases) instead of single words provides PSMT with a high degree of robustness in word selection and in local-word reordering. Recent developments have shown that improvements in PSMT quality are possible using syntax. One such development is the pre-translation reordering approach, which adjusts the source sentence to resemble target-language word order prior to translation. This is typically done using rules that are either manually created or automatically learned from word-aligned parallel corpora.

One particular variety of this approach, proposed by Elming (2008), uses a large set of linguistic features to automatically learn reordering rules. The rules are applied non-deterministically; however, phrase-internal word-alignments are used to ensure that the intended reordering does not come undone because of phrase internal reordering (Elming, 2008). This approach was shown to produce improved MT output on English-Danish MT, a relatively closely-related and similarly-structured language pair. In this paper, we study whether this approach can be extended to distant language pairs, specifically English-to-Arabic. We achieve significant improvement in translation quality over related approaches, measured by manual as well as automatic evaluations on this task. This proves the viability of this approach on distant languages. We also examined the effect of the alignment method on learning reordering rules. Interestingly, our experiments produced better translation using rules learned from automatic alignments than using rules learned from manual alignments.

In the next section, we discuss and contrast related work. Section 3 describes aspects of English and Arabic structure that are relevant to reordering. Section 4 describes the automatic induction of reordering rules and its integration in PSMT. In section 5, we describe the SMT system used in the experiments. In section 6, we evaluate and discuss the results of our English-Arabic MT system.

2 Related Work

Much work has been done in syntactic reordering for SMT, focusing on both source and target-language syntax. In this paper, we adapt an approach that utilizes source-syntax information as opposed to target-side syntax systems (Yamada and Knight, 2001; Galley et al., 2004). This is because we are translating from English to Arabic and we are discouraged by recent results indicating Arabic parsing is not at a stage that makes it usable in MT (Habash et al., 2006). While several recent authors using a pre-translation (source-side) reordering approach have achieved positive results, it has been difficult to integrate syntactic

Proceedings of the EACL 2009 Workshop on Computational Approaches to Semitic Languages, pages 69–77,
Athens, Greece, 31 March, 2009.

information while retaining the strengths of the statistical approach. In some studies, reordering decisions are done "deterministically" by supplying the decoder with a canonical word order (Xia and McCord, 2004; Collins et al., 2005; Wang et al., 2007; Habash, 2007). These reordering rules are either manually specified or automatically learned from alignments; and they are always placed outside the actual PSMT system. By contrast, other studies (Crego and Mariño, 2007; Zhang et al., 2007; Li et al., 2007; Elming, 2008) are more in the spirit of PSMT, in that multiple reorderings are presented to the PSMT system as (possibly weighted) options that are allowed to contribute alongside other parameters. Specifically, we follow the pre-translation reordering approach of Elming (2008). This approach has been proven to remedy shortcomings of other pre-translation reordering approaches by reordering the input word sequence, but scoring the output word sequence.

Elming (2008) only examined the approach within English – Danish, a language pair that displays little reordering. By contrast, in this paper, we target the more demanding reordering task of translating between two distant languages, English and Arabic. While much work has been done on Arabic to English MT (Habash and Sadat, 2006; Lee, 2004) mostly focusing on addressing the problems caused by the rich morphology of Arabic, we handle the less described translation direction: English to Arabic. Recently, there are some new publications on English to Arabic MT. Sarikaya and Deng (2007) use joint morphological-lexical language models to re-rank the output of English dialectal-Arabic MT, and Badr et al. (2008) report results on the value of the morphological decomposition of Arabic during training and describe different techniques for re-composition of Arabic in the output. We differ from the previous efforts targeting Arabic in that (1) we do not address morphology issues through segmentation (more on this in section 3) and (2) we focus on utilizing syntactic knowledge to address the reordering challenges of this translation direction.

3 Arabic Syntactic Issues

Arabic is a morphologically and syntactically complex language with many differences from English. Arabic morphology has been well studied in the context of MT. Previous results all suggest that some degree of tokenization is helpful when translating from Arabic (Habash and Sadat, 2006; Lee, 2004). However, when translating into a morphologically rich language, target tokenization means that the translation process is broken into multiple steps (Badr et al., 2008). For our experiments, Arabic was not segmented apart from simple punctuation tokenization. This low level of segmentation was maintained in order to agree with the segmentation provided in the manually aligned corpus we used to learn our rules (section 6.1). We found no simple means for transferring the manual alignments to more segmented language. We expect that better performance would be achieved by introducing more Arabic segmentation as reported by Badr et al. (2008).[1] As such, and unlike previous work in PSMT translating into Arabic, we focus here on syntax. We plan to investigate different tokenization schemes for syntactic preprocessing in future work. Next, we describe three prominent English-Arabic syntactic phenomena that have motivated some of our decisions in this paper.

First is verb-subject order. Arabic verb subjects may be: (a.) pro-dropped (verb conjugated), (b.) pre-verbal (SVO), or (c.) post-verbal (VSO). Although the English SVO order is possible in Arabic, it is not always preferred, especially when the subject is particularly long. Unfortunately, this is the harder case for PSMT to handle. For small subject noun phrases (NP), PSMT might be able to handle the reordering in the phrase table if the verb and subject were seen in training. But this becomes much less likely with very long NPs that exceed the size of the phrases in a phrase table. The example in Figure 1 illustrates this point. Bolding and italics are used to mark the verb and subordinating conjunction that surround the subject NP (19 tokens) in English and what they map to in Arabic, respectively.[2]

Secondly, Arabic adjectival modifiers typically follow their nouns with the exception of some superlative adjectives. However, English adjectival modifiers can follow or precede their nouns depending on the size of the adjectival phrase: single word adjectives precede but multi-word adjectives phrases follow (or precede while hyphenated). For example, *a tall man* translates as رجل طويل *rjl*

[1] Our results are not comparable to their results, since they report on non-standard data sets.

[2] All Arabic transliterations in this paper are provided in the Habash-Soudi-Buckwalter scheme (Habash et al., 2007).

[NP-SBJ The general coordinator of the railroad project among the countries of the Gulf Cooperation Council , Hamid Khaja ,] **[V announced]** *[SUB that ...]*

[V اعلن] [NP-SBJ المنسق العام لمشروع السكة الحديد بين دول مجلس التعاون الخليجي حامد خاجه] [SUB ان ...]

[V Aςln] [NP-SBJ Almnsq AlςAm lmšrwς Alskħ AlHdyd byn dwl mjls AltςAwn Alxlyjy HAmd xAjh] *[SUB An ...]*

Figure 1: An example of long distance reordering of English SVO order to Arabic VSO order

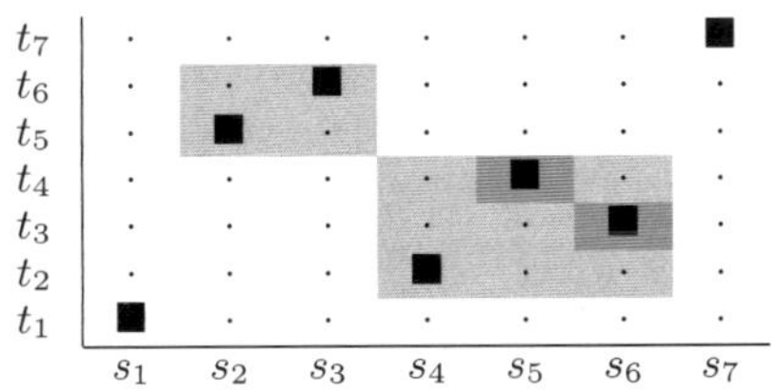

Figure 2: Abstract alignment matrix example of reordering.

Twyl 'man tall'; however, the English phrase *a man tall of stature* translates with no reordering as رجل طويل القامة *rjl Twyl AlqAmħ* 'man tall the-stature'. So does the superlative *the tallest man* translating into اطول رجل *ATwl rjl* 'tallest man.'

Finally, Arabic has one syntactic construction, called *Idafa*, for indicating possession and compounding, while English has three. The Idafa construction typically consists of one or more indefinite nouns followed by a definite noun. For example, the English phrases *the car keys*, *the car's keys* and *the keys of the car* all translate into the Arabic مفاتيح السيارة *mfAtyH AlsyArħ* 'keys the-car.' Only one of the three English constructions does not require content word reordering.

4 Reordering rules

4.1 Definition of reordering

Following Elming (2008), we define reordering as two word sequences, left sequence (LS) and right sequence (RS), exchanging positions. These two sequences are restricted by being parallel consecutive, maximal and adjacent. The sequences are not restricted in length, making both short and long distance reordering possible. Furthermore, they need not be phrases in the sense that they appear as an entry in the phrase table.

Figure 2 illustrates reordering in a word alignment matrix. The matrix contains reorderings between the light grey sequences (s_2^3 and s_4^6)[3] and the dark grey sequences (s_5^5 and s_6^6). On the other hand, the sequences s_3^3 and s_4^5 are not considered for reordering, since neither one is maximal, and s_4^5 is not consecutive on the target side.

4.2 Learning rules

Table 1 contains an example of the features available to the algorithm learning reordering rules. We include features for the candidate reordering sequences (LS and RS) and for their possible left (LC) and right (RC) contexts. In addition to words and parts-of-speech (POS), we provide phrase structure (PS) sequences and subordination information (SUBORD). The PS sequence is made up of the highest level nodes in the syntax tree that cover the words of the current sequence and only these. Subordinate information can also be extracted from the syntax tree. A subordinate clause is defined as inside an SBAR constituent; otherwise it is a main clause. Our intuition is that all these features will allow us to learn the best rules possible to address the phenomena discussed in section 3 at the right level of generality.

In order to minimize the amount of training data, word and POS sequences are annotated as too long (T/L) if they are longer than 4 words, and the same for phrase structure (PS) sequences if they are longer than 3 units. A feature vector is only used if at least one of these three levels is not T/L for both LS and RS, and T/L contexts are not included in the set. This does not constrain the possible length of a reordering, since a PS sequence of length 1 can cover an entire sentence. In the example in Table 1, LS and RS are single words, but they are not restricted in length. The span of the contexts varies from a single neighboring word to all the way to the sentence border. In the example, LS and RS should be reordered, since adjectives appear as post-modifiers in Arabic.

In order to learn rules from the annotated data, we use a rule-based classifier, Ripper (Cohen,

[3] Notation: s_x^y means the consecutive source sequence covering word positions x to y.

<table>
<tr><th>Level</th><th>LC</th><th>LS</th><th>RS</th><th>RC</th></tr>
<tr><td>WORD</td><td><s> he bought || he bought || bought</td><td>new</td><td>books</td><td>today || today . || today . < /s></td></tr>
<tr><td>POS</td><td><S> NN VBD || NN VBD || VBD</td><td>JJ</td><td>NNS</td><td>NN || NN . || NN . < /S></td></tr>
<tr><td>PS</td><td><S> NP VBD || NP VBD || VBD</td><td>JJ</td><td>NNS</td><td>NP || NP . || NP . < /S></td></tr>
<tr><td>SUBORD</td><td>MAIN</td><td>MAIN</td><td>MAIN</td><td>MAIN</td></tr>
</table>

Table 1: Example of features for rule-learning. Possible contexts separated by ||.

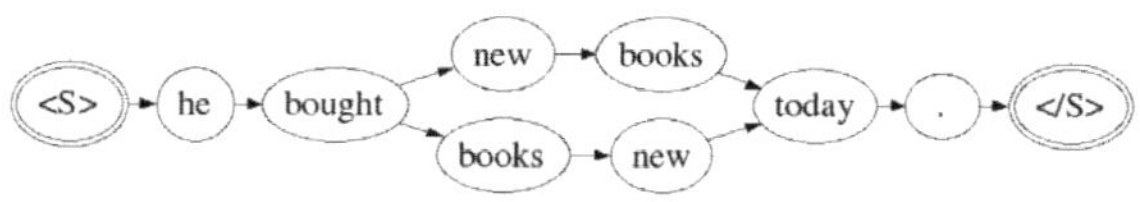

Figure 3: Example word lattice.

1996). The motivation for using Ripper is that it allows features to be sets of strings, which fits well with our representation of the context, and it produces easily readable rules that allow better understanding of the decisions being made. In section 6.3, extracted rules are exemplified and analyzed.

The probabilities of the rules are estimated using Maximum Likelihood Estimation based on the information supplied by Ripper on the performance of the individual rules on the training data. These logarithmic probabilities are easily integratable in the log-linear PSMT model as an additional parameter by simple addition.

5 The PSMT system

Our baseline is the PSMT system used for the 2006 NAACL SMT workshop (Koehn and Monz, 2006) with phrase length 3 and a trigram language model (Stolcke, 2002). The decoder used for the baseline system is Pharaoh (Koehn, 2004) with its distance-penalizing reordering model. Since Pharaoh does not support word lattice input, we use our own decoder for the experiments. Except for the reordering model, it uses the same knowledge sources as Pharaoh, i.e. a bidirectional phrase translation model, a lexical weight model, phrase and word penalties, and a target language model. Its behavior is comparable to Pharaoh when doing monotone decoding.

The search algorithm of our decoder is similar to the RG graph decoder of (Zens et al., 2002). It expects a word lattice as input. Figure 3 shows the word lattice for the example in table 2. In the example used here, we choose to focus on the reordering of adjective and noun. For readability, we do not describe the possibility of reordering the subject and verb. This will also be the case in later use of the example.

Since the input format defines all possible word orders allowed by the rule set, a simple monotone search is sufficient. Using a language model of order n, for each hypothesized target string ending in the same n-1-gram, we only have to extend the highest scoring hypothesis. None of the others can possibly outperform this one later on. This is because the maximal context evaluating a phrase extending this hypothesis, is the history (n-1-gram) of the first word of that phrase. The decoder is not able to look any further back at the preceding string.

5.1 The reordering approach

Similar to Elming (2008), the integration of the rule-based reordering in our PSMT system is carried out in two separate stages:

1. Reordering the source sentence to assimilate the word order of the target language.
2. Weighting of the target word order according to the rules.

Stage (1) is done in a non-deterministic fashion by generating a word lattice as input. This way, the system has both the original word order, and the reorderings predicted by the rule set. The different paths of the word lattice are merely given as equal suggestions to the decoder. They are in no way individually weighted.

Separating stage (2) from stage (1) is motivated by the fact that reordering can have two distinct origins. They can occur because of stage (1), i.e. the lattice reordering of the original English word order (phrase *external* reordering), and they can occur inside a single phrase (phrase *internal* reordering). The focus of this approach lies in doing *phrase-independent* word reordering. Rule-predicted reorderings should be promoted regardless of whether they owe their existence to a syntactic rule or a phrase table entry.

This is accomplished by letting the actual scoring of the reordering focus on the target string.

Source:	he_1 $bought_2$ new_3 $books_4$ $today_5$	
Rule:	$3\ 4 \rightarrow 4\ 3$	
Hypothesis	Target string	Alignment
H1	Aštrý jdydħ ktbA	1+2 3 4
H2	Aštrý ktbA jdydħ	1+2 4 3

Table 2: Example of the scoring approach during decoding at source word 4.

The decoder is informed of where a rule has predicted a reordering, how much it costs to do the reordering, and how much it costs to avoid it. This is then checked for each hypothesized target string via a word alignment.

The word alignment keeps track of which source position the word in each target position originates from. In order to access this information, each phrase table entry is annotated with its internal word alignment, which is available as an intermediate product from phrase table creation. If a phrase pair has multiple word alignments, the most frequent one is chosen.

Table 2 exemplifies the scoring approach, again with focus on the adjective-noun reordering. The source sentence is *'he bought new books today'*, and a rule has predicted that source word 3 and 4 should change place. Due to the pro-drop nature of Arabic, the first Arabic word is linked to the two first English words (1+2). When the decoder has covered the first four input words, two of the hypothesis target strings might be H1 and H2. At this point, it becomes apparent that H2 contains the desired reordering (namely what corresponds to source word order '4 3'), and it get assigned the reordering cost. H1 does not contain the rule-suggested reordering (instead, the words are in the original order '3 4'), and it gets the violation cost. Both these scorings are performed in a phrase-independent manner. The decoder assigns the reordering cost to H2 without knowing whether the reordering is internal (due to a phrase table entry) or external (due to a syntactic rule).

Phrase internal reorderings at other points of the sentence, i.e. points that are not covered by a rule, are not judged by the reordering model. Our rule extraction does not learn every possible reordering between the two languages, but only the most general ones. If no rule has an opinion at a certain point in a sentence, the decoder is free to choose the phrase translation it prefers without reordering cost.

Separating the scoring from the source language reordering also has the advantage that the approach in essence is compatible with other approaches such as a traditional PSMT system (Koehn et al., 2003b) or a hierarchical phrase system (Chiang, 2005). We will, however, not examine this possibility further in the present paper.

6 Evaluation

6.1 Data

We learn the reordering rules from the IBM Arabic-English aligned corpus (IBMAC) (Ittycheriah and Roukos, 2005). Of its total 13.9K sentence pairs, we only use 8.8K sentences because the rest of the corpus uses different normalizations for numerals that make the two sets incompatible. 6.6K of the sentences (179K English and 146K Arabic words) are used to learn rule, while the rest are used for development purposes. In addition to the manual alignment supplied with these data, we create an automatic word alignment for them using GIZA++ (Och and Ney, 2003) and the *grow-diag-final* (GDF) symmetrization algorithm (Koehn et al., 2005). This was done together with the data used to train the MT system. The English side is parsed using a state-of-the-art statistical English parser (Charniak, 2000). Two rule sets are learned based on the manual alignments (MAN) and the automatic alignments (GDF).

The MT system is trained on a corpus consisting of 126K sentences with 4.2M English and 3.3M Arabic words in simple tokenization scheme. The domain is newswire (LDC-NEWS) taken from Arabic News (LDC2004T17), eTIRR (LDC2004E72), English translation of Arabic Treebank (LDC2005E46), and Ummah (LDC2004T18). Although there are additional corpora available, we restricted ourselves to this set to allow for a fast development cycle. We plan to extend the data size in the future. The Arabic language model is trained on the 5.4M sentences (133M words) of newswire text in the 1994 to 1996 part of the Arabic Gigaword corpus. We restricted ourselves to this part, since we are not able to run Pharaoh with a larger language model.[4]

For test data, we used NIST MTEval test sets from 2004 (MT04) and 2005 (MT05)[5]. Since these data sets are created for Arabic-English evaluation with four English reference sentences for

[4] All of the training data we use is available from the Linguistic Data Consortium (LDC): http://www.ldc.upenn.edu/.

[5] http://www.nist.gov/speech/tests/mt/

System		Dev	MT04	MT05
Pharaoh Free		28.37	23.53	24.79
Pharaoh DL4		29.52	24.72	25.88
Pharaoh Monotone		27.93	23.55	24.72
MAN	NO weight	29.53	24.72	25.82
	SO weight	29.43	24.74	25.82
	TO weight	29.40	24.78	25.93
GDF	NO weight	29.87	25.11	26.04
	SO weight	29.84	25.06	26.01
	TO weight	29.95	25.17	26.09

Table 3: Automatic evaluation scores for different systems using rules extracted from manual alignments (MAN) and automatic alignments (GDF). The TO system using GDF rules is significantly better than the light grey cells at a 95% confidence level (Zhang et al., 2004).

each Arabic sentence, we invert the sets by concatenating all English sentences to one file. This means that the Arabic reference file contains four duplicates of each sentence. Each duplicate is the reference of a different English source sentence. Following this merger, MT04 consists of 5.4K sentences with 193K English and 144K Arabic words, and MT05 consists of 4.2K sentences with 143K English and 114K Arabic words. MT04 is a mix of domains containing speeches, editorials and newswire texts. On the other hand, MT05 is only newswire.

The NIST MTEval test set from 2002 (MT02) is split into a tuning set for optimizing decoder parameter weights and a development set for ongoing experimentation. The same merging procedure as for MT04 and MT05 is employed. This results in a tune set of 1.0K sentences with 34K English and 26K Arabic words, and a development set of 3.1K sentences with 102K English and 79K Arabic words.

6.2 Results and discussion

The reordering approach is evaluated on the MT04 and MT05 test sets. Results are listed in table 3 along with results on the development set. We report on (a) Pharaoh with no restriction on reordering (Pharaoh Free), (b) Pharaoh with distortion limit 4 (Pharaoh DL4), (c) Pharaoh with monotone decoding (Pharaoh Monotone), and (d) a system provided with a rule reordered word lattice but no (NO) weighting in the spirit of (Crego and Mariño, 2007), (e) the same system but with a source order (SO) weighting in the spirit of (Zhang et al., 2007; Li et al., 2007), and finally (f) the same system but with the target order (TO) weighting.

System	MT04	MT05	Avr. human
Pharaoh Free	24.07	25.15	3.0 (2.80)
Pharaoh DL4	25.42	26.51	—
NO scoring	25.68	26.29	2.5 (2.43)
SO scoring	25.42	26.02	2.5 (2.64)
TO scoring	25.98	26.49	2.0 (2.08)

Table 4: Evaluation on the diff set. Average human ratings are medians with means in parenthesis, lower scores are better, 1 is the best score.

In addition to evaluating the reordering approaches, we also report on supplying them with different reordering rule sets: a set that was learned on manually aligned data (MAN), and a set learned on the same data but with automatic alignments (GDF).

6.2.1 Overall Results

Pharaoh Monotone performs similarly to Pharaoh Free. This shows that the question of improved reordering is not about quantity, but rather quality: what constraints are optimal to generate the best word order. The TO approach gets an increase over Pharaoh Free of 1.3 and 1.6 %BLEU on the test sets, and 0.2 and 0.5 %BLEU over Pharaoh DL4.

Improvement is less noticeable over the other pre-translation reordering approaches (NO and SO). A possible explanation is that the rules do not apply very often, in combination with the fact that the approaches often behave alike. The difference in SO and TO scoring only leads to a difference in translation in ~14% of the sentences. This set, the *diff* set, is interesting, since it provides a focus on the difference between these approaches. In table 4, we evaluate on this set.

6.2.2 Diff Set

Overall the TO approach seems to be a superior reordering method. To back this observation, 50 sentences of MT04 are manually evaluated by a native speaker of Arabic. Callison-Burch et al. (2007) show that ranking sentences gives higher inter-annotator agreement than scoring adequacy and fluency. We therefore employ this evaluation method, asking the evaluator to rank sentences from four of the systems given the input sentence. Ties are allowed. Table 4 shows the average rat-

	Decoder choice	NO	SO	TO
MT04	Phrase internal	20.7	0.6	21.2
	Phrase external	30.1	43.0	33.1
	Reject	49.2	56.5	45.7
MT05	Phrase internal	21.3	0.7	21.6
	Phrase external	29.5	42.9	31.8
	Reject	49.2	56.4	46.5

Table 5: The reordering choices made based on the three pre-translation reordering approaches for the 20852 and 17195 reorderings proposed by the rules for the MT04 and MT05 test sets. Measured in %.

ings of the systems. This shows the TO scoring to be significantly superior to the other methods ($p < 0.01$ using Wilcoxon signed-rank testing).

6.2.3 MAN vs GDF

Another interesting observation is that reordering rules learned from automatic alignments lead to significantly better translation than rules learned from manual alignment. Due to the much higher quality of the manual alignment, the opposite might be expected. However, this may be just a variant on the observation that alignment improvements (measured against human references) seldom lead to MT improvements (Lopez and Resnik, 2006). The MAN alignments may in fact be better than GDF, but they are most certainly more different in nature from real alignment than the GDF alignments are. As such, the MAN alignments are not as powerful as we would have liked them to be. In our data sets, the GDF rules, seem less specific, and they therefore apply more frequently than the MAN rules. On average, this results in more than 7 times as many possible reordering paths per sentence. This means that the GDF rules supply the decoder with a larger search space, which in turn means more proposed translation hypotheses. This may play a big part in the effect of the rule sets.

6.2.4 Reordering Choices

Table 5 shows the reordering choices made by the approaches in decoding. Most noticeable is that the SO approach is strongly biased against phrase internal reorderings; TO uses more than 30 times as many phrase internal reorderings as SO. In addition, TO is less likely to reject a rule proposed reordering.

The 50 sentences from the manual evaluation are also manually analyzed with regards to reordering. For each reordering in these sentences, the four systems are ranked according to how well the area affected by the reordering is translated. This indicates that the SO approach's bias against phrase internal reorderings may hurt performance. 25% of the time, when SO chooses an external reordering, while the TO approach chooses an internal reordering, the TO approach gets a better translation. Only in 7% of the cases is it the other way around.

Another discovery from the analysis is when TO chooses an internal reordering and NO rejects the reordering. Here, TO leads to a better translation 45% of the time, while NO never outperforms TO. In these cases, either approach has used a phrase to cover the area, but via rule-based motivation, TO has forced a less likely phrase with the correct word order through. This clearly shows that local reordering is not handled sufficiently by phrase internal reordering alone. These need to be controlled too.

6.3 Rule analysis

The rule learning resulted in 61 rules based on manual alignments and 39 based on automatic alignments. Of these, the majority handled the placement of adjectives, while only a few handled the placement of the verb.

A few of the rules that were learned from the manual alignment are shown in table 6. The first two rules handle the placement of the finite verb in Arabic. Rule 16 states that if a finite verb appears in front of a subordinate clause, then it should be moved to sentence initial position with a probability of 68%. Due to the restrictions of sequence lengths, it can only swap across maximally 4 words or a sequence of words that is describable by maximally 3 syntactic phrases. The SBAR condition may help restrict the reordering to finite verbs of the main clause. This rule and its probability goes well with the description given in sections 3, since VSO order is not obligatory. The subject may be unexpressed, or it may appear in front of the verb. This is even more obvious in rule 27, which has a probability of only 43%.

Rules 11 and 1 deal with the inverse ordering of adjectives and nouns. The first is general but uncertain, the second is lexicalized and certain. The reason for the low probability of rule 11 is primarily that many proper names have been mis-tagged by the parser as either JJ or NN, and to a lesser

No	LC	LS	RS	RC	Prob.
16	WORD: <s>		POS: FVF	PS: SBAR	68%
27	WORD: <s>	PS: NP	POS: FVF		43%
11	POS: IN	POS: JJ	POS: NN		46%
1	! POS: JJ	POS: JJ	WORD: president		90%
37	! POS: NN ! POS: JJ	POS: NN	POS: NNS	POS: IN	71%

Table 6: Example rules. ! specifies negative conditions.

extent that the rule should often not apply if the right context is also an NN. Adding the latter restriction narrows the scope of the rule but would have increased the probability to 54%.

Rule 1, on the other hand, has a high probability of 90%. It is only restricted by the condition that the left context should not be an adjective. In these cases, the adjectives should often be moved together, as is the case with *'the south african president'* → الرئيس الجنوب افريقي *Alrŷys Aljnwb Afryqy* where *'south african'* is moved to the right of *'president'*.

Finally, rule 37 handles compound nouns. Here a singular noun is moved to the right of a plural noun, if the right context is a preposition, and the left context is neither an adjective nor a singular noun. This rule handles compound nouns, where the modifying function of the first noun often is hard to distinguish from that of an adjective. The left context restrictions server the same purpose as the left context in rule 1; these should often be moved together with the singular noun. The function of the right context is harder to explain, but without this restriction, the rule would have been much less successful; dropping from a probability of 71% to 51%.

An overall comparison of the rules produced based on the manual and automatic alignments shows no major difference in quality. This is especially interesting in light of the better translation using the GDF rules. It is also very interesting that it seems possible to get as good rules from the GDF as from the MAN alignments. This is a new result compared to Elming (2008), where results on manual alignments only are reported.

7 Conclusion and Future Plans

We have explored the syntactic reordering approach previously presented in (Elming, 2008) within a more distant language pair, English-Arabic. A translation direction that is highly under-represented in MT research, compared to the opposite direction. We achieve significant improvement in translation quality over related approaches, measured by manual as well as automatic evaluations on this task. Thus proving the viability of the approach on distant languages.

We also examined the effect of the alignment method on learning reordering rules. Interestingly, our experiments produced better translation using rules learned from automatic alignments than using rules learned from manual alignments. This is an aspect we want to explore further in the future.

In future work, we would also like to address the morphological complexity of Arabic together with syntax. We plan to consider different segmentations for Arabic and study their interaction with translation and syntactic reordering.

An important aspect of the TO approach is that it uses phrase internal alignments during translation. In the future, we wish to examine the effect their quality has on translation. We are also interested in examining the approach within a standard phrase-based decoder such as Moses (Koehn et al., 2003b) or a hierarchical phrase system (Chiang, 2005).

The idea of training on reordered source language is often connected with pre-translation reordering. The present approach does not employ this strategy, since this is no trivial matter in a non-deterministic, weighted approach. Zhang et al. (2007) proposed an approach that builds on unfolding alignments. This is not an optimal solution, since this may not reflect their rules. Training on both original and reordered data may strengthen the approach, but it would not remedy the problems of the SO approach, since it would still be ignorant of the internal reorderings of a phrase. Nevertheless, it may strengthen the TO approach even further. We also wish to examine this in future work.

References

I. Badr, R. Zbib, and J. Glass. 2008. Segmentation for English-to-Arabic statistical machine translation. In *Proceedings of ACL'08: HLT, Short Papers*, Columbus, OH, USA.

C. Callison-Burch, C. Fordyce, P. Koehn, C. Monz, and J. Schroeder. 2007. (Meta-) evaluation of machine translation. In *Proceedings of ACL'07 Workshop on Statistical Machine Translation*, Prague, Czech Republic.

E. Charniak. 2000. A maximum-entropy-inspired parser. In *Proceedings of NAACL'00*, Seattle, WA, USA.

D. Chiang. 2005. A hierarchical phrase-based model for statistical machine translation. In *Proceedings of ACL'05*, Ann Arbor, MI, USA.

W. Cohen. 1996. Learning trees and rules with set-valued features. In *Proceedings of AAAI*, Portland, OR, USA.

M. Collins, P. Koehn, and I. Kucerova. 2005. Clause restructuring for statistical machine translation. In *Proceedings of ACL'05*, Ann Arbor, MI, USA.

J. M. Crego and J. B. Mariño. 2007. Syntax-enhanced n-gram-based smt. In *Proceedings of the MT Summit*, Copenhagen, Denmark.

J. Elming. 2008. Syntactic reordering integrated with phrase-based smt. In *Proceedings of the ACL Workshop on Syntax and Structure in Statistical Translation (SSST-2)*, Columbus, OH, USA.

M. Galley, M. Hopkins, K. Knight, and D. Marcu. 2004. What's in a translation rule? In *Proceedings of HLT/NAACL'04*, Boston, MA, USA.

N. Habash and F. Sadat. 2006. Arabic preprocessing schemes for statistical machine translation. In *Proceedings of HLT-NAACL'06*, New York, NY, USA.

N. Habash, B. Dorr, and C. Monz. 2006. Challenges in Building an Arabic-English GHMT System with SMT Components. In *Proceedings of AMTA'06*, Cambridge, MA, USA.

N. Habash, A. Soudi, and T. Buckwalter. 2007. On Arabic Transliteration. In A. van den Bosch and A. Soudi, editors, *Arabic Computational Morphology: Knowledge-based and Empirical Methods*. Springer.

N. Habash. 2007. Syntactic preprocessing for statistical machine translation. In *Proceedings of the MT Summit*, Copenhagen, Denmark.

A. Ittycheriah and S. Roukos. 2005. A maximum entropy word aligner for arabic-english machine translation. In *Proceedings of EMNLP*, Vancouver, Canada.

P. Koehn and C. Monz. 2006. Manual and automatic evaluation of machine translation between European languages. In *Proceedings of the Workshop on Statistical Machine Translation at NAACL'06*, New York, NY, USA.

P. Koehn, F. J. Och, and D. Marcu. 2003a. Statistical phrase-based translation. In *Proceedings of NAACL'03*, Edmonton, Canada.

P. Koehn, F. J. Och, and D. Marcu. 2003b. Statistical Phrase-based Translation. In *Proceedings of NAACL'03*, Edmonton, Canada.

P. Koehn, A. Axelrod, A. Birch Mayne, C. Callison-Burch, M. Osborne, and D. Talbot. 2005. Edinburgh system description for the 2005 IWSLT speech translation evaluation. In *International Workshop on Spoken Language Translation 2005 (IWSLT'05)*, Pittsburgh, PA, USA.

P. Koehn. 2004. Pharaoh: a beam search decoder for phrase-based statistical machine translation models. In *Proceedings of AMTA'04*, Washington, DC, USA.

Y. Lee. 2004. Morphological Analysis for Statistical Machine Translation. In *Proceedings of HLT-NAACL'04*, Boston, MA, USA.

C. Li, M. Li, D. Zhang, M. Li, M. Zhou, and Y. Guan. 2007. A probabilistic approach to syntax-based reordering for statistical machine translation. In *Proceedings of ACL'07*, Prague, Czech Republic.

A. Lopez and P. Resnik. 2006. Word-based alignment, phrase-based translation: what's the link? In *Proceedings of AMTA'06*, Cambridge, MA, USA.

F. J. Och and H. Ney. 2003. A systematic comparison of various statistical alignment models. *Computational Linguistics*, 29(1):19–51.

R. Sarikaya and Y. Deng. 2007. Joint morphological-lexical language modeling for machine translation. In *Proceedings of HLT-NAACL'07, Short Papers*, Rochester, NY, USA.

A. Stolcke. 2002. Srilm – an extensible language modeling toolkit. In *Proceedings of the International Conference on Spoken Language Processing*, Denver, CO, USA.

C. Wang, M. Collins, and P. Koehn. 2007. Chinese syntactic reordering for statistical machine translation. In *Proceedings of EMNLP-CoNLL*, Prague, Czech Republic.

F. Xia and M. McCord. 2004. Improving a statistical mt system with automatically learned rewrite patterns. In *Proceedings of COLING'04*, Geneva, Switzerland.

K. Yamada and K. Knight. 2001. A Syntax-Based Statistical Translation Model. In *Proceedings of ACL'01*, Toulouse, France.

R. Zens, F. J. Och, and H. Ney. 2002. Phrase-based statistical machine translation. In M. Jarke, J. Koehler, and G. Lakemeyer, editors, *KI - 2002: Advances in Artificial Intelligence. 25. Annual German Conference on AI*. Springer Verlag.

Y. Zhang, S. Vogel, and A. Waibel. 2004. Interpreting bleu/nist scores: How much improvement do we need to have a better system? In *Proceedings of the 4th International Conference on Language Resources and Evaluation (LREC'04)*, Lisbon, Portugal.

Y. Zhang, R. Zens, and H. Ney. 2007. Improved chunk-level reordering for statistical machine translation. In *Proceedings of the IWSLT*, Trento, Italy.

Author Index